J.M. BARRIE

James Matthew Barrie was born in Scotland in 1860. After graduating from Edinburgh University, he worked as a journalist, writing his first novel, *Better Dead*, in 1887. After some success in Scotland with his fiction, Barrie moved to London to pursue his career as a playwright in the 1890s.

He married actress Mary Ansell in 1894, but it was not to be a happy union and they eventually divorced in 1909. It was while escaping his troubled home life in the late 1890s, walking in Kensington Gardens, that he met the Llewelyn Davies brothers, and in them found the inspiration for his best-known work, *Peter Pan*. Barrie was to be made guardian of the Llewelyn Davies boys following the death of their parents.

Peter Pan first appeared in Barrie's 1902 novel *The Little White Bird*. The stage play of *Peter Pan* delighted London audiences when it premiered in 1904, and was a huge success for Barrie. His novel based on the play, *Wendy and Peter*, was published in 1911, to rave reviews.

Barrie continued to write fiction and plays, though his later work was aimed mainly at adults, and his novels *The Twelve-Pound Look* (1910) and *Half an Hour* (1913) contained distinctly darker elements than his earlier writings.

Barrie died in 1937. In his will, he bequeathed the copyright of *Peter Pan* to Great Ormond Street Children's Hospital in London. Peter, the Lost Boys, Wendy, Captain Hook and all the denizens of Neverland live on in countless much-loved stage and screen adaptations, ensuring that Peter Pan really is the boy that will never grow up.

ELLA HICKSON

Ella Hickson's debut play *Eight* (Bedlam Theatre, Edinburgh) won a Fringe First Award, the Carol Tambor 'Best of Edinburgh' Award and was nominated for an Evening Standard Award. It transferred to the Trafalgar Studios, London, and PS122, New York. Her other plays include *Precious Little Talent* (Bedlam Theatre, Edinburgh, and Trafalgar Studios, London); *Hot Mess* (Hawke & Hunter, Edinburgh, and Latitude Festival); *Soup* (Òran Mór at Traverse Theatre, Edinburgh); *PMQ* (Theatre503 and HighTide Festival); *Boys* (HighTide Festival, Nuffield Theatre, Southampton and Soho, London) and *The Authorised Kate Bane* (Grid Iron at Traverse Theatre, Edinburgh, and Tron Theatre, Glasgow). She completed a creative writing MA at the University of Edinburgh and spent a year working with the Traverse Theatre as their Emerging Playwright on Attachment. She was the 2011 Pearson Playwright in Residence for the Lyric Hammersmith and is the recipient of the 2013 Catherine Johnson Award.

Ella is under commission to Headlong Theatre and the Almeida Theatre. Her short film *Hold On Me* (dir. Samuel Abrahams) premiered at the 55th BFI London Film Festival and she is currently developing new projects with Mammoth Screen, Company and Endor.

Ella Hickson

WENDY
& PETER PAN

Adapted from the book by
J. M. Barrie

NICK HERN BOOKS
London
www.nickhernbooks.co.uk

ABOUT THE ROYAL SHAKESPEARE COMPANY

The Shakespeare Memorial Theatre opened in Stratford-upon-Avon in 1879. Since then the plays of Shakespeare have been performed here, alongside the work of his contemporaries and of modern playwrights. In 1960 the Royal Shakespeare Company was formed, gaining its Royal Charter in 1961.

The founding Artistic Director, Peter Hall, created an ensemble theatre company of young actors and writers. The Company was led by Hall, Peter Brook and Michel Saint-Denis. The founding principles were threefold: the Company would embrace the freedom and power of Shakespeare's work, train and develop young actors and directors and, crucially, experiment in new ways of making theatre. There was a new spirit amongst this post-war generation and they intended to open up Shakespeare's plays as never before.

The impact of Peter Hall's vision cannot be underplayed. In 1955 he premiered Samuel Beckett's *Waiting for Godot* in London, and the result was like opening a window during a storm. The tumult of new ideas emerging across Europe in art, theatre and literature came flooding into British theatre. Hall channelled this new excitement into the setting up of the Company in Stratford. Exciting breakthroughs took place in the rehearsal room and the studio day after day. The RSC became known for exhilarating performances of Shakespeare alongside new masterpieces such as *The Homecoming* and *Old Times* by Harold Pinter. It was a combination that thrilled audiences.

Peter Hall's rigour on classical text became legendary, but what is little known is that he applied everything he learned working on Beckett, and later on Harold Pinter, to his work on Shakespeare, and likewise he applied everything he learned from Shakespeare onto modern texts. This close and exacting relationship between writers from different eras became the fuel which powered the creativity of the RSC.

The search for new forms of writing and directing was led by Peter Brook. He pushed writers to experiment. "Just as Picasso set out to capture a larger slice of the truth by painting a face with several eyes and noses, Shakespeare, knowing that man is living his everyday life and at the same time is living intensely in the invisible world of his thoughts and feelings, developed a method through which we can see at one and the same time the look on a man's face and the vibrations of his brain."

In our fifty years of producing new plays, we have sought out some of the most exciting writers of their generation. These have included: Edward Albee, Howard Barker, Edward Bond, Howard Brenton, Marina Carr, Caryl Churchill, Martin Crimp, David Edgar, Helen Edmundson, James Fenton, Georgia Fitch, David Greig, Dennis Kelly, Tarell Alvin McCraney, Martin McDonagh, Frank McGuinness, Rona Munro, Anthony Neilson, Harold Pinter, Phil Porter, Mike Poulton, Mark Ravenhill, Adriano Shaplin, Tom Stoppard, debbie tucker green and Roy Williams.

The Company today is led by Gregory Doran, whose recent appointment represents a long-term commitment to the disciplines and craftsmanship required to put on the plays of Shakespeare. He, along with Executive Director, Catherine Mallyon, and his Deputy Artistic Director, Erica Whyman, will take forward a belief in celebrating both Shakespeare's work and the work of his contemporaries, as well as inviting some of the most exciting theatre-makers of today to work with the Company on new plays.

The RSC Ensemble is generously supported by THE GATSBY CHARITABLE FOUNDATION and THE KOVNER FOUNDATION.

The RSC is grateful for the significant support of its principal funder, Arts Council England, without which our work would not be possible. Around 50 per cent of the RSC's income is self-generated from Box Office sales, sponsorship, donations, enterprise and partnerships with other organisations.

Supported using public funding by

ARTS COUNCIL ENGLAND

NEW WORK AT THE RSC

We are a contemporary theatre company built on classical rigour. Through an extensive programme of research and development, we resource writers, directors and actors to explore and develop new ideas for our stages, and as part of this we commission playwrights to engage with the muscularity and ambition of the classics and to set Shakespeare's world in the context of our own. In 2015 we will reopen The Other Place, our studio theatre in Stratford-upon-Avon, which will be a creative home for new work and experimentation. Leading up to that reopening we will continue to find spaces and opportunities to offer our audiences contemporary voices alongside our classical repertoire.

We invite writers to spend time with us in our rehearsal rooms, with our actors and practitioners. Alongside developing their own plays for our stages, we invite them to contribute dramaturgically to both our main stage Shakespeare productions and our work for young people. We believe that engaging with living writers and other contemporary theatre makers helps to establish a creative culture within the Company which both inspires new work and creates an ever more urgent sense of enquiry into the classics. Shakespeare was a great innovator and breaker of rules, as well as a bold commentator on the times in which he lived. It is his spirit of 'Radical Mischief' which informs new work at the RSC.

Erica Whyman, Deputy Artistic Director, heads up this strand of the Company's work, Pippa Hill is our Literary Manager and Mark Ravenhill is our Playwright in Residence.

The RSC British Playwright in Residence is generously supported by the Columbia Foundation Fund of The Capital Community Foundation.

The RSC Literary Department is generously supported by THE DRUE HEINZ TRUST.

CROSS is the exclusive pen partner of the RSC in support of New Work.

This production of *Wendy & Peter Pan* was first performed by the
Royal Shakespeare Company in the Royal Shakespeare Theatre,
Stratford-upon-Avon, on 10 December 2013. The cast was as follows:

WENDY	**Fiona Button**
JOHN	**Jolyon Coy**
MICHAEL	**Brodie Ross**
TOM	**Colin Ryan**
MRS DARLING	**Rebecca Johnson**
MR DARLING	**Andrew Woodall**
DOC GILES	**Arthur Kyeyune**
PETER	**Sam Swann**
TINK	**Charlotte Mills**
TOOTLES	**Josh Williams**
NIBS	**Jack Monaghan**
CURLY	**Dafydd Llyr Thomas**
SLIGHTLY	**Will Merrick**
CAPTAIN HOOK	**Guy Henry**
SMEE	**Gregory Gudgeon**
DOC SWAIN	**Guy Rhys**
KNOCK BONE JONES	**Richard Clews**
MURT THE BAT	**Dodger Phillips**
SKYLIGHTS	**Andrew Woodall**
MARTIN	**Jamie Wilkes**
TIGER LILY	**Michelle Asante**
CROCODILE	**Arthur Kyeyune**
SHADOWS	**Simon Carroll-Jones**
	Matt Costain
	Arthur Kyeyune
	Susan Hingley
	Emily Holt
	Jack Horner

Directed by	**Jonathan Munby**
Designed by	**Colin Richmond**
Lighting Designed by	**Oliver Fenwick**
Music by	**Olly Fox**
Sound by	**Christopher Shutt**
Movement by	**Michael Ashcroft**
Fights by	**Terry King**
Video Designed by	**Ian William Galloway**
Aerial Consultant	**Matt Costain**
Company Text and Voice Work by	**Nia Lynn**
Assistant Director	**Caroline Byrne**
Music Director	**Bruce O'Neil**
Assistant Music Director	**Candida Caldicot**
Casting by	**Hannah Miller** CDG **Annelie Powell**
Literary Manager	**Pippa Hill**
Production Manager	**Peter Griffin**
Costume Supervisor	**Sabine Lemaître**
Company Manager	**Jondon**
Stage Manager	**Francis Lynch**
Deputy Stage Manager	**Carol Pestridge**
Assistant Stage Manager	**Emma McKie**

MUSICIANS

Flutes	**Ian Reynolds**
Clarinets	**Rela Spyrou**
Violin	**Samantha Norman**
Trumpet	**Andrew Stone Fewings**
Guitar	**Liz Larner**
Percussion	**Kevin Waterman**
Percussion	**Joelle Barker**
Keyboard	**Bruce O'Neil**

This text may differ slightly from the play as performed.

LOVE THE RSC

Support us and make a difference

The RSC is a registered charity. We perform all year round in our Stratford-upon-Avon home, as well as having regular seasons in London, and touring extensively within the UK and overseas for international residencies.

By supporting us through RSC Membership or joining the Supporters' Ensemble you will help to fund our work both on and off the stage.

Choose a level that suits you from £18 through to £10,000 per year and enjoy a closer connection with the RSC, whilst at the same time enabling us to continue to make the theatre that you love.

For more information visit **www.rsc.org.uk/supportus** or call the RSC Membership Office on 01789 403440.

WENDY & PETER PAN

Ella Hickson

Adapted from the book by J.M. Barrie

For Elizabeth,

May you have the best of adventures.

Magic does exist. I promise.

Come away, O human child!
To the waters and the wild
With a faery, hand in hand
For the world's more full of weeping
Than you can understand.

'The Stolen Child'
W. B. Yeats

In memory of Christopher,
and all the other lost boys and girls – play on

6

Characters

WENDY
JOHN
MICHAEL
TOM
MRS DARLING
MR DARLING
DOC GILES
PETER
TINK
TOOTLES
NIBS
CURLY
SLIGHTLY
CAPTAIN HOOK
SMEE
DOC SWAIN
KNOCK-BONE JONES
FIRST MATE MURT THE BAT
SKYLIGHTS
MARTIN THE CABIN BOY
TIGER LILY
THE CROCODILE

Plus SHADOWS, PIRATES

This text went to press before the end of rehearsals and so may differ slightly from the play as performed.

ACT ONE

Scene One

1908: the Darling children's nursery – a winter afternoon. We can see the steeples and rooftops of London in the distance. A game of ambush is underway; the troops are in their hiding positions. JOHN, eleven, camouflaged and rather serious, has his target in his sights. MICHAEL, ten, clumsy and conflict-averse, has his hands over his teddy's ears and TOM, six and utterly fearless, teeters on the point of action.

JOHN (*hushed*). Hunker down, chaps, rifles at the ready – the beasts are in the undergrowth.

MICHAEL. What?

JOHN (*accompanied by selection of ridiculous hand signals*). The red squirrel is concealing his snout.

TOM. I'm not sure I understand.

JOHN. Shhh! Get down! On my signal, it's going to be 'Bye Bye Crimea!' Weapons at the ready, boys!

MICHAEL (*jumps up from his hiding position*). Surely we could try and reach some kind of diplomatic solution before /

JOHN (*infuriated, also jumping up*). / It's a battle, Michael.

MICHAEL. But must battle be so – fighty? Why can't we play at talking it through or agreeing nicely or shaking hands or /

JOHN *snaps a branch off Planty (a plant).* MICHAEL *is in shock.*

That was rather aggressive, John. I'm not sure I liked it.

JOHN *throws his bow on the floor in rage.*

JOHN. Right, Tom – you're promoted to first brother. Come on, up front.

TOM. But Michael's older.

JOHN. Take Michael's sword.

TOM. Wendy said we had to remember to do our homework before we played battle.

JOHN. We're soldiers, we're battling, we have *far* more important things to be thinking about than homework.

MICHAEL. Perhaps the soldiers are doing their homework in preparation for battle? Or… they've just come back and they're all bloody and sweaty and tired and they think 'Ooh – maybe I'll have a little rest and do a nice spot of quiet homework'?

JOHN (*booming*). *Back* to your positions! Rifles at the ready! Targets in sights!

TOM *and* MICHAEL *jump back to their positions.*

On three: one – two /

JOHN *inhales ready to give the 'go' –* WENDY, *twelve, scruffy-haired and big-hearted, blusters in.*

WENDY. / John, your football kit is getting mouldy by the back door and, Michael, Mother said you had to… Tom – that button is falling off, come here and I'll – (*Looking at the scene.*) Oooh – are you playing battles? Can I play? Please can I? Please? Please?

JOHN. No nags allowed on the battlefield.

WENDY. I'm not a nag. Mother asked me to ask you – I /

JOHN *plonks* WENDY *in the chair and ties her up roughly.*

JOHN. / Fine, you can be the damsel and that's all. Men, new objective, save the damsel before scalping the natives. Everybody clear?

WENDY. I just need to sew Tom's button on.

JOHN. Wendy, are you a damsel or are you a button-sewer?

WENDY. I'm a damsel but /

JOHN. / Okay, well – damsels must be very very scared, then very very impressed, then very very grateful. No button-sewing necessary.

TOM. Maybe you could do my button afterwards?

JOHN. Don't reveal your position!

TOM. I was being, am being – oh, I find it very hard.

    MICHAEL *giggles*.

JOHN. Soldiers do not giggle!

    TOM *coughs*.

    No coughing.

    TOM *coughs*.

    Insubordination! Insubordination!

    WENDY *laughs*.

    No giggling!

WENDY (*trying to restrain herself*). Sorry – sorry very sorry.

JOHN. You're fired!

MICHAEL (*charging*). Fiiiiiire! Fiiiiiire!

TOM. Fire!!

    TOM *charges*. JOHN *abandons control and in a desperate plea for victory, launches himself at the bed – it's joyous, raucous, they're laughing – then suddenly* JOHN *knocks a bedside lamp and it comes crashing to the floor. All four children stop and stand, shame-faced.*

    Did I win?

JOHN. Thomas Darling, I can not believe you just broke Mother's lamp.

WENDY. You broke the lamp.

    JOHN *picks up the lamp and goes to hide it in the drawer.*

MICHAEL. You can't just hide it.

    TOM *coughs*.

JOHN. Fine – we'll do the proper thing – fine. Okay?

    JOHN *puts the lamp on the floor and bows his head.*

In war, some men must fall; this lamp has made the greatest sacrifice, we commit this lamp to the 'Don't Tell Mother' drawer with great sadness.

WENDY *starts making the 'dum dum di dum' of a funeral march*. JOHN *rests the broken lamp in the 'Don't Tell Mother' drawer, overflowing with broken toys*. MRS DARLING, *out on the landing, listens in*, MR DARLING *surprises her – twists her round and kisses her, they smile*.

MRS DARLING. What was that for?

MR DARLING. Wanted to.

MR DARLING *looks at* MRS DARLING.

MRS DARLING. What?

MR DARLING. There's a kiss that hides right here in the corner of your mouth and I can never quite get at it.

MRS DARLING. Why, George – I don't know what you mean.

MR DARLING. You are the most delicious riddle.

MR DARLING *takes* MRS DARLING *in his arms and they dance a little, they laugh – they kiss again*.

MRS DARLING. Shall we check on our children; I think there's a little high jinks going on.

MR DARLING *and* MRS DARLING *enter the nursery*.

I believe I heard something smash.

JOHN. No.

MR DARLING. Wendy?

WENDY (*opens her mouth and makes a funny throaty snotty sound*). I can't lie – snotfrogs come out when I try.

MR DARLING (*stern*). Did you lie, John?

JOHN. I may have done. A little bit.

MRS DARLING. Did you smash the lamp?

JOHN. Yes.

MRS DARLING. Well then, I hope you don't mind missing your pocket money for three weeks.

The children look solemnly at their feet.

MR DARLING. If you have been careless enough to break the lamp then… (*Whispers.*) where's the genie?

MRS DARLING. George?

MRS DARLING *rolls her eyes but gives in to the fun.* MR DARLING *puts a lampshade on his head and does some sort of ridiculous Cossack dance.*

MR DARLING. It is wrote, the lamp is broke, a puff of smoke – then alacazam and alaberoo – I have three wishes I grant to youuu!

The children, delighted, run at their father and hug him furiously.

WENDY. Chocolate, books and mice!

JOHN. Lava, scorpions and pork pies!

MICHAEL. Plants, frogs and taffeta!

JOHN. Michael?

MICHAEL. What?

JOHN. Taffeta? Urgh.

TOM *coughs.*

MRS DARLING. Tom? Are you all right?

TOM *nods.*

TOM. I'd just like cake. I can't think of another two – once cake is in your head it's very difficult to think of anything else.

MR DARLING (*silly accent*). But listen here, my little fishes, there are only three wishes, so we must see who can stand the most…

CHILDREN (*squeal and try to escape*). No – please – no!

MR DARLING. TICKLES!!

MR DARLING *captures all the children at the same time and tickles them furiously, the children squeal and squirm; it is a picture of the happiest of families.*

MRS DARLING. Come on! Cake time! Downstairs!

MR DARLING. Last one to the table is a jibbering jubber-dummy!

MICHAEL *and* JOHN *race out of the room past* MR DARLING. *He turns to follow them and they exit.* TOM *coughs.* MRS DARLING *scoops him up.*

MRS DARLING. Tom, you're not all right – you're not all right at all; you're burning up.

WENDY. Tom?

MRS DARLING. Wendy, go and tell Father to call for Dr Giles. Now!

WENDY *exits and returns and cowers to see the lights lower and the room get dark, shadows grow tall up the walls.* MRS DARLING *rocks* TOM *in a nursing chair and hums a haunting tune.* DOC GILES *enters. His hat is leather, suggesting eyes and nostrils perhaps, his cloak long and shiny as if recently emerged from some nearby swamp – his doctor's case a dark-green crocodile skin, its jaws snapping open and revealing sharp instruments within. The* DOC(*odile*) *takes little* TOM*'s tiny arm in his and we hear the loud 'tick-tock, tick-tock' of his pocket watch as it is held out to mark the child's weakening pulse. He takes the stethoscope, a little like a reptile's tongue, and holds it to the child's chest.* WENDY *picks up* TOM*'s button and looks longingly at it.*

WENDY. Tom… your button – I forgot.

Lights down.

Scene Two

The nursery is quiet and dark. MRS DARLING *sleeps in an armchair by* TOM's *bed.* WENDY, JOHN *and* MICHAEL *are asleep in their beds.* TOM's *nightlight glows. The wind blows. The nursery window creaks open. In tiny moments, seen only by flashes of light from a fairy that lingers by his side – the face of* PETER PAN. *He's at the window, on a table, and then by* TOM's *bed.* PETER *plays an eerie tune on his harmonica and suddenly he's surrounded by an army of* SHADOWS. *The silent troupe hovers by* TOM's *bed before lifting him up – up and away – out of the window and off into the night.* PETER *remains behind a moment, he catches sight of* WENDY's *face and he can't tear himself away.* MRS DARLING *rouses – the fairy grabs* PETER *and drags him out of the window. With a flurry, the window closes and above the nursery – in the night sky a new star appears; the smallest and brightest star in the sky.* TINK's *light darts across the sky followed by the* SHADOW *of* PETER PAN.

MRS DARLING *rouses.*

MRS DARLING. Tom? Tom.

Scene Three

Winter, 1909 – we are one year on. WENDY *is getting* JOHN
and MICHAEL *into bed. The window is slightly open. The
nursery is darker now, more sombre.* MICHAEL *is sitting on
the floor playing with a toy boat.* WENDY *stands at the window
looking out into the night.*

MICHAEL. Why do you keep staring out of the window?

WENDY. I'm sure I keep seeing a boy, or maybe the shadow
  of a –

JOHN. Wendy, you've gone totally gaga.

WENDY. No I haven't.

JOHN. Lost it, box of frogs – we'll have to put you in an
  asylum.

WENDY. Michael, into bed.

MICHAEL. I want Mother to tuck me in.

WENDY. Well, you've got me.

MICHAEL. Can we play pirates? You can be Captain and I
  can be /

  JOHN *takes* MICHAEL*'s boat from him and drops it in the
  bin, he picks up his book and gets into bed.*

JOHN. I'm reading.

MICHAEL. Can you tell me a story?

JOHN. There once was a boy called John who died from always
  being asked annoying questions; the end.

MICHAEL. Wendy, John's being /

WENDY. / John, have you washed behind your ears?

  JOHN *licks his hand and wipes it behind his ears.*

  Ugh, you're disgusting.

JOHN. I'm meant to be disgusting – I'm a boy.

MICHAEL. Fine, I'll play on my own.

MICHAEL exits into the bathroom. MRS DARLING is in her housedress about to enter the nursery. MR DARLING catches her. MR DARLING is dressed smartly and now sports an incredibly large and rather ridiculous-looking moustache.

MR DARLING. Why aren't you ready?

MRS DARLING. I don't feel up to it, George.

MR DARLING. Please get dressed.

MRS DARLING. You go and I'll /

MR DARLING. / We haven't been to one work function this season; do you know how that looks?

MRS DARLING. I'd imagine it looks like something's wrong.

Beat.

MR DARLING. It's been a year, Mary. How long are we going to /

MRS DARLING. / 'We'? You seem to be perfectly fine.

MR DARLING. I'm just trying to /

MRS DARLING. / I'm going to say goodnight to my children.

MR DARLING exits. MRS DARLING enters the nursery. WENDY leaps up to her feet and leans out of the window.

WENDY. There! Look! I knew it! Look!

MRS DARLING. Wendy, come away from that window!

WENDY. He's there, Mother. I swear – I /

MRS DARLING. / Close it. I won't have you getting a chill.

WENDY. I promise – I just saw him, he was flying.

MRS DARLING comes over and closes the window and marches WENDY into her bed.

MRS DARLING. No more of these stories. Lights out;
Michael, John, you too, tuck in.

MICHAEL *re-enters wearing a towel on his head. He waters
Planty by his bed – strokes it goodnight and climbs under the
covers.* MR DARLING *enters, trying to do up his tie
and failing.*

MR DARLING. This blasted tie. Mary – we need to go.

MRS DARLING. I haven't given their children their medicine.

MR DARLING. They're not unwell. Michael, take that off your
head at once.

MICHAEL. But I'm a mermaid.

MR DARLING. Off.

WENDY. What if Father gives us our medicine and then,
Mother, you can go and get ready?

MRS DARLING *looks at her daughter – who has such good
will in her face.*

MRS DARLING. What a good idea. (*Aside to* MR DARLING
as she goes.) You'd have a better chance of tying that if you
could see straight, George.

MRS DARLING *exits.* MICHAEL *stands.*

MICHAEL. I'm just saying now, before there's any further talk
about it; I won't be taking my medicine.

MR DARLING. Wendy, show Michael.

WENDY. Mm it's yummy. Aghhhuuu. Snotfrogs – sorry.

MICHAEL. See.

MR DARLING. Be a man, Michael.

WENDY. You should show Michael how brave you are in
taking yours.

WENDY *reaches into her father's inside pocket and pulls
out a hip flask.*

MR DARLING. No, no – it's different to your medicine.

MICHAEL. Father's a cowardy custard.

JOHN. Father!

MR DARLING. Mother will be so upset if you don't take yours, please, Michael.

MICHAEL. Only if you take yours.

MR DARLING. I can't I /

WENDY. / One – two – three –

MR DARLING. Okay, look – just quickly – there.

MRS DARLING *enters,* MR DARLING *swigs.*

MRS DARLING. George, what are you doing?

MR DARLING. I – I –

WENDY. It's his medicine; he was showing us how brave he is.

MRS DARLING. No, he was being the biggest coward of all.

MRS DARLING *strides past* MR DARLING, *snubbing him, and heads to tuck* MICHAEL *in.*

MICHAEL. Mother – I'm so glad of you. Will you kiss Planty too?

MRS DARLING. Of course.

MRS DARLING *kisses the plant and goes over to* JOHN.

Goodnight, my little soldier.

MRS DARLING *kisses* WENDY *on the head.*

WENDY. Will you and Father be friends again?

MRS DARLING. Don't you worry about any of that; sleep tight.

MRS DARLING *goes upstage to check that the window is firmly closed. She gets a little distracted by a small star shining particularly bright this evening.* MR DARLING *watches his wife and turns away.*

MR DARLING. Goodnight, children. Mary, we should be off.

JOHN/MICHAEL. Goodnight, Father.

WENDY. Father?

MR DARLING. Yes?

WENDY *stands on the end of her bed so that she is face to face with her father. She plays with his face, smoothes his moustache.*

WENDY. I don't know if this thing is a very good idea. I miss your top lip.

MR DARLING. But it's all the rage.

WENDY. Silly Daddy. (*Does up her father's bow tie for him.*) All done.

WENDY *kisses her father on the end of his nose.* MRS DARLING *catches sight.*

MR DARLING. Thank you.

WENDY. I think you're very brave.

MR DARLING. Bedtime.

MR DARLING *tucks* WENDY *in.* MRS DARLING *joins* MR DARLING. *They stop at the door, thinking the children can't hear them but* WENDY, *still awake, creeps forward and listens in.*

We need to go to this party.

MRS DARLING. 'Need'?

MR DARLING. We need to have some fun.

MRS DARLING. What I need is distraction, purpose. If I sit here I can do nothing but think of him.

MR DARLING. There is a bowl of invitations downstairs; the Blundens, the Bedfords, the Seddons and the Hawthornes – a christening, a ball, two weddings – and not one of them taken up! And you complain of lack of company?

MRS DARLING. I cannot have one more conversation about the colour of a lampshade, or the price of baby's bonnet, or the seemingly endless details of Mr Bennett's disobedient digestive tract!

Beat.

MR DARLING. I can see that you're overtired; perhaps you should have a lie-down.

MRS DARLING. Bog off, George.

MR DARLING. I have to go to /

MRS DARLING. / Then go.

MR DARLING *exits*. MRS DARLING *exits*.

Scene Four

In the nursery, WENDY, *who has been listening to her parents at the door, takes the nightlight, sets it on the ground.*

WENDY (*half-whisper, half-prayer*). I know I shouldn't complain, and I know it will get better in time but I am trying so hard – and I just can't – keep... pfff – (*Trying not to cry.*) Look, Tom, if you're there? If you're out there – please, help me – please help it get better – because I – I – John is so angry he's broken three trains and Michael gets so nervous that he can't get his words out at school and Mother and Father... don't laugh, ever any more – (*Beat.*) and I don't know how to... how to...

The window flies open, the gust of wind blows WENDY's *candle out. There is a storm brewing, lightning and thunder, the windows clatter and then – in a gust – in tumbles* PETER. *It is not a glamorous entrance, he trips, he stumbles and he lands in a heap behind one of the beds. Behind him a ball of light.*

(*Dashing over.*) Oh, Tom, it's you – oh, Tom! I'm so glad you came back – oh, Tom!

PETER (*still concealed*). Ow – my bum.

PETER *pops up his head up from the bed,* WENDY *and* PETER *lock eyes for the first time.*

(*Suddenly love-struck.*) Hello. Hi.

WENDY. You're not Tom.

PETER. Bump.

WENDY. What?

PETER. Ow – I bump-ed – nothing to do with my –

WENDY. Bum.

PETER. No.

Suddenly there is a jangling of bells and a bright light zooms past PETER, he catches it and throws it into a jug, trapping it. The jug shakes violently. WENDY grabs a teddy bear and wields it as if it's a weapon at PETER and the jug.

WENDY. Okay, all right – get back – what is that? Who are you?

PETER removes a large dagger from his boot and wields it at WENDY.

Oh – okay, okay – no.

WENDY drops the bear. PETER lowers the dagger, picks up the bear and offers it to WENDY, gently – who takes it hesitantly and holds it to her.

Thanks.

WENDY goes to touch PETER to see if he is real, but PETER pulls back.

PETER. No. No one touches me. Not ever. You've got a lovely biscuit face. What? I'm going to go now.

PETER turns to go, embarrassed.

WENDY. I'm Wendy – Wendy Moira Angela Darling.

WENDY steps towards PETER and PETER steps back.

Are you afraid of girls?

PETER (*stepping forward boldly*). No. I'm not afraid of anything.

WENDY steps back from him.

Are you afraid of boys?

WENDY. Not normally. But you –

PETER. Are particularly terrifying.

WENDY. No –

PETER. Very savage.

WENDY. No.

PETER. Incredibly brave.

WENDY. You've broken into my bedroom in the middle of the night. It's – creepy.

PETER. I haven't broken in; a-a-actually, I fell.

WENDY. What were you doing outside?

PETER. Looking.

WENDY. Still creepy. Creepier – in fact.

PETER. No – I – I've come to collect something – my shadow.

WENDY. Your shadow?

PETER. Yes.

WENDY. You can't leave your shadow; shadows stay stuck.

PETER. Yours stays stuck but that's because you're not a Lost Boy.

WENDY. A what?

PETER (*starts searching, sniffing angrily about the place*). A shadow, a good-for-nothing, disloyal, un-sticky, pain in the /

WENDY. / Lost boy? How do you know that we lost a boy?

Beat. PETER *realises he's let something slip – he panics. A jug on the side starts to shake violently. Out of the jug explodes a bright white light –* PETER *catches it in his hands as it zooms across the room and successfully stuffs it into a toy box, which he then sits on. It rattles.*

What was that?

The toy box rattles furiously.

PETER. Hm?

WENDY. Is that your shadow?

PETER. No – no – *that's* my shadow!

PETER *suddenly spots something under one of the beds – he leaps and pulls his* SHADOW *out from under the bed by its toe, there's a tussle but* PETER *has him.*

WENDY. Wow – that's – amazing – he's completely separate and still all – shadowy. How is that…

WENDY *walks around the* SHADOW, *transfixed.* PETER *likes that she's impressed.*

PETER. I've got more.

WENDY. More than one shadow?

PETER. I got loads. You want to see?

WENDY *nods, excited –* PETER *takes out his harmonica and plays an eerie tune – in through the window come bowling a team of* SHADOWS. WENDY *backs away.*

WENDY. Whoa, whoa – Wait, wait – tell me who you are right now or I'll scream.

The SHADOWS *all point to themselves.*

No – you – bum boy – with the hair.

The SHADOWS *disappear.*

How did you? Where did they – they've gone? Who are you?

PETER (*suddenly soaring up – up into the sky, it's magic*). I'm Pan. Pirate killer, prince of the seas, demon of the skies – the most savage, the incredible, unbeatable and blinking majestical – (*Lands with suave charm.*) Peter Pan.

WENDY *looks up at him. He smiles a cheeky smile.*

WENDY. That's… amazing.

PETER. You don't sound very amazed.

WENDY. I thought the – the boy who's been at the window… I thought it was someone else. Not you.

PETER. Who?

WENDY. No one, it doesn't matter, it – was stupid of me.

PETER *clambers down;* WENDY *sits sadly on the side of the bed,* PETER *comes over.*

PETER. It looks like your face might rain. Please don't rain, biscuit face, you'll go all soggy.

WENDY *looks up into* PETER*'s face, they lock eyes – for a moment it might be a kiss.*

WENDY. I'm going to scream now, if that's okay?

PETER. Really?

WENDY. You said that you were a savage killer or something so – I should probably…

PETER. Six out of seven dwarves aren't happy.

WENDY. What?

PETER. Trying to make you laugh.

WENDY. Still going to scream.

PETER. Right. Um… I – um –

WENDY *takes a deep breath in.* PETER *doesn't know what to do, he's all at a loss, arms flailing, trying to sort of patch* WENDY *but unsure how.* WENDY *looks at him struggling and smiles softly – she laughs a little.*

WENDY. You all right?

PETER. Yeah.

WENDY. What are you doing?

PETER. Um… I was um trying to – make it better. I think.

PETER *tries to lean against something and stumbles.* WENDY *laughs.*

WENDY. 'The most savage'?

PETER. I tripped.

WENDY. Over your shadow?

PETER'S SHADOW *laughs with* WENDY.

PETER. On my shoelace.

WENDY. You're not wearing any shoes.

PETER. None of the Lost Boys wear /

WENDY. / Lost boys. There, again – lost boys, how do you know – you know where they are, don't you?

PETER. No.

WENDY. No, no! You will tell me what you know right now! Stop! Peter – stop!

PETER. I – I can't – I'm sorry – I –

WENDY. Tell me!

PETER. I'm sorry – I can't!

PETER *blows and the window opens, and he dodges past* WENDY.

WENDY. I'll give you a kiss.

PETER (*turning suddenly*). A kiss?

WENDY. If you're going to be a boy about it.

PETER. A kiss? Really?

WENDY. Yes, but only because you are quite…

PETER. Quite what?

WENDY. Do you want one or not?

PETER *puts out his hand. The* SHADOW *looks away, embarrassed.*

Oh.

WENDY, *confused, stares at the hand.* WENDY *grabs a thimble from her dress pocket and puts it in* PETER*'s hand.*

PETER. Now I must give you a kiss.

WENDY. That wasn't the deal.

PETER *picks up a button off the side – the same button that* WENDY *was meant to sew onto* TOM*'s jumper.*

A button? (*Looks at it a moment, rather sadly.*) Sorry, no –
a kiss. There we go; done. Now – where I can find the lost
boys?

PETER. I gave you a kiss. I – gave you – a girl – a kiss – and it
went fine. Right? You thought it was okay? I mean, I don't –
care – obviously – but you know, on average, you'd say – it
went well, right?

WENDY. I'll take it back if you don't tell me.

PETER. Lost Boys live in Neverland.

PETER *says it and claps his hand over his mouth. The toy
box shakes violently and out screams the bright light and a
wild jangling of bells.* PETER *catches the light and wrestles
it into the wardrobe – he desperately tries to keep the
wardrobe shut behind him but he can't, the jangling of bells
gets louder and louder.* JOHN *sits up in bed.*

JOHN. Look here, I don't like being woken up by – who is he?
Wendy?

WENDY. Peter, what is in there?

PETER. When the first baby laughed for the first time its laugh
broke into a thousand tiny pieces and they all went skipping
about and that was the beginning of –

Out of the wardrobe explodes a human-sized fairy. TINK *is
a tubby little cockney tinker – think Big Fat Gypsy Tink –
her hair piled up on her head, large hooped earrings and a
dress, made out of a skeleton leaf, frayed at the edges and
tight round the bust, with perhaps a whisper of an Adidas
stripe in it.*

Fairies.

WENDY. That's one thousandth of a baby's laugh?

JOHN. Jolly big baby.

TINK (*straight at* WENDY). You calling me fat? Hm?

WENDY. No –

TINK. Glass houses, love, I'm not the one in the nightdress kissing boys I never met before, now am I?

JOHN. Kissing? What? Where? No.

PETER. This is Tink; she gets big when she's full of feeling. Tink, this is Wendy. Be nice.

TINK. Enchanted. (*Aside to* PETER.) Peter, we need to leave *immediately*.

WENDY. You can't.

JOHN (*standing up on his bed*). Look here, I don't know who you two think you are or what you're doing in my bedroom 'talking' to my sister, but unless you leave in two seconds I'll –

JOHN *draws his toy sword on* PETER. PETER *somersaults majestically and lands on the end of* JOHN's *bed and crows.*

WENDY (*dreamily, laughing, enchanted*). John – this is Peter Pan. He's going to take us to Neverland to find our lost boy.

JOHN. I don't like him.

WENDY. Come on, Michael – wake up!

TINK. Flaming Nora! No he is not!

MICHAEL (*climbing out of bed, putting on his glasses and being very polite*). Good evening, Flaming Nora, it is a pleasure to meet you. Your dress appears to be a leaf of the genus Quercus, would you mind awfully if I /

TINK. / Keep your genus and your Quercus to yourself, mate.

JOHN. No – look, wait. I'm not going on one of Wendy's 'adventures'. I've taken all the crochet and cake-making and hair-brushing one brother can take, okay? So 'Neverland' with its pretty pink ponies can do one – as can you, young man.

PETER. Ponies? Mermaids –

MICHAEL. Mermaids!?

PETER. Pirates and Never Wolves and fairy orgies and…

JOHN. Pirates? Really?

PETER. Most evil pirate in the world lives on Neverland. (*Something comes over* PETER, *a little like a trance*.) Black heart, red eyes, foulest barnacled buccaneer you've ever smelt. Picks the flesh of children out from between his teeth with his... hook.

JOHN. H-h-hook? You know Captain Hook?

MICHAEL. You've *seen* him?

PETER. Who do you think sliced off his hand and fed it to the crocodile?

MICHAEL. No?

JOHN. For God's sake, Wendy, stop faffing; Peter's waiting. She's so slow, Peter, it's a nightmare.

TINK. Peter, a word.

WENDY. It was really you?

PETER *inhales ready to regale* WENDY *with the story when* TINK *grabs him and pulls him away.*

TINK. You can't – you can't do this – Pete.

WENDY. I thought no one could touch him?

TINK. I'm a fairy, it's different – now keep ya beak out. Peter – just think about it – she tells her family and they'll put us in a jar or a box or worse – stick a tree up my /

PETER. / How can she tell them? She'll be in Neverland. Just think how pleased the boys will be when they see I've brought them a mother!

TINK. Mother? You are kiddin'? What's got into you?

PETER. I'm just being kind and helping this poor girl find her brother.

TINK. Oh hark, my tiny violin – you know as well as I do he ain't on Neverland yet and taking her there lookin' is only slowing it down.

PETER. Look – I just – I want to and I'm Captain and so what I want /

WENDY. / We're ready, Peter.

PETER. Great – you can't carry things though, you'll need your arms for flying.

TINK. Oh for – (*Flips out – storms off.*)

MICHAEL. Fly? We can't fly.

TINK. Oh dear, *quel dommage* – Prissy, Dippy and Dopey won't be going after all.

JOHN. Flying? Pff – piece of cake – just show me how, picked up ruggers in a jiffy.

PETER. You just have to think one happy thought. One completely happy thought – think it till it fills up your whole head and your feet will just lift right up off the ground.

The Darling children try – very hard – but can't seem to do it.

MICHAEL. I can't find one.

WENDY. It's been a long year.

JOHN (*sulking*). I don't see why I need to have a happy thought to scalp a pirate.

PETER. Tink, give them fairy dust.

TINK. I'm telling you, Pete – this is a –

JOHN *swipes at the dust – and it goes all over him.*

Oi! You little – !

MICHAEL. Me! Me too!

TINK *begrudgingly sprinkles* MICHAEL.

WENDY. Me, me – do me.

PETER. Tink.

JOHN. Can't feel a thing.

TINK *throws fairy dust in* WENDY's *face.*

MICHAEL. Oh, I feel very odd – my face is all tingly.

JOHN. Your face is always tingly.

MICHAEL. No it is not!

JOHN (*mocking*). 'Oh, my face is all tingly, my legs are all wobbly, my personality is all *soggy*.'

MICHAEL. My personality is not all /

JOHN. / Oh, stop being such a girl, Michael – it's not doing any…

JOHN, MICHAEL *and* WENDY *start lifting up into the air.*

Oh – oh!

WENDY (*holding on to the bed*). No – I – really, it's silly, actually. All this is… very immature – Peter!

PETER. The bed can't come to – let go.

WENDY. I don't want to – I'm scared. (*Lifts so high she is forced to let go of the bed.*) Oh! Oh!

JOHN. Mummy! Mummy! I mean funny – ha – feels awfully funny!

MICHAEL. The ground is getting very far away!

PETER. Tink; lead the way!

JOHN. I'll navigate – I've got a very good sense of direction, inaugural Scout. Got my toggle in no time! Peter, throw me a bearing, old chap!

PETER. Second on the right and straight on till morning!

JOHN. I think you'll find that's actually /

TINK. / Pipe down, gobby, and follow me!

PETER *grabs* WENDY's *hand and together they soar up. He grins at her – he's got her. She grins back. The ceiling of the bedroom pulls away and the children are exposed to the night sky, full of stars and speckled with snow. The five voyagers zoom upwards circling the nursery – as if they are a five-figure mobile. Their night lights become beacons*

*throwing animals and landscapes up and round the walls. As
the children circle, the nursery transforms… The four-poster
beds grow up into trunks and sprout leaves – the canopies
above the beds stretch out to become the starry night sky,
the rocking horse gallops off into the undergrowth, the
chandelier grows vines, dropping down and sprouting the
most amazing coloured flowers, creeping its way through
the forest.*

WENDY. It's amaaazing! It's totally, oh look – it's brilliant!
Oh, Peter!

WENDY *shoots him a grin. He grins back.*

I'm going to find Tom!

PETER. Hold on!

The children exit.

ACT TWO

Scene One

We are in the clearing in the middle of the Never Forest – there is a fine mist hanging low. The PIRATES *seep into the scene, they are out hunting* LOST BOYS *– yellow skin and wild eyes, half-monster half-man, they come creeping…* DOC SWAIN *with his peg-leg and doctor's bag of torture tools,* KNOCK-BONE JONES *skinny-malinky and wonky-stepped,* FIRST MATE MURT THE BAT, *blind in one eye,* MARTIN THE CABIN BOY, *red-headed, pale-skinned with a runny nose, and* SKYLIGHTS, *a croaky old storyteller.*

PIRATES.
>Find them boys and string 'em up.
>Find 'em, blind 'em – Take their guts.
>Find them boys and break their legs –
>Boil 'em, oil 'em – smash their heads,
>Knife 'em, slice 'em – clean in two –
>Skin 'em, trim 'em – make fish food.
>Fi /

DOC SWAIN raises his hand, the pack freezes and hunkers.

DOC SWAIN. / Shh – I can smell the stink of children. We're near!

The PIRATES *spread out and sniff, snarling near the faces of the little ones in the crowd.*

JONES. We're going to kill 'em and skin 'em, sauté their little limbs and serve 'em to the Captain on a platter!

MURT. Well, we'd better get it done before dusk; else another one of us is losing a digit.

MURT holds up his hand and a finger is missing.

DOC SWAIN. Stop bleatin' – this way.

SKYLIGHTS. It's been weeks since I got my hands bloody, I'm gasping for a fight.

PIRATES. Aaaarrghh.

MURT tries to light his pipe. The others look on awkwardly – his blind eye gives him no depth perception so he keeps missing the pipe with the match.

MURT. Ouch. You sure, Swain? We got lost three times already cos you thought you got a sniff.

DOC SWAIN. What you saying?

MURT. I'm saying, those boys are 'arder to find than an ant's bollock on a beach.

DOC SWAIN. Just keep an eye out, eh, Murt?

JONES. Will you two /

MURT. / Careful we don't have to leg it, Swain.

DOC SWAIN pulls a cleaver on MURT. MURT pulls his sword on DOC SWAIN.

JONES. Shh! You hear that? There's a rustle – a – a –

The PIRATES all freeze and draw their swords.

MARTIN sneezes violently – the PIRATES all jump out of their skin.

MARTIN. I'm sorry, I'm sorry – I'm so sorry – it's my hay fever, my eyes are streaming – my nose is like a tap, it's all this undergrowth, it's hellish.

MURT tries to light his pipe again.

DOC SWAIN. Someone help him, for Christ's sake.

JONES. We ain't got time for this! If we don't get those boys before dusk – I need all my fingers!

MARTIN lights it for him, MURT goes to slap him on the back in thanks and misses him completely. MARTIN sneezes again. SKYLIGHTS grabs MARTIN and snarls at him.

MARTIN. We need to keep looking else the Captain will – the Captain will /

SKYLIGHTS. / Ooh, you're going a bit pink.

MARTIN. Really? Where? But I used factor fifty?

SKYLIGHTS. You think you can tell me about our Captain, do ya, schoolboy?

JONES. Leave him be, we got work to do.

SKYLIGHTS. Captain James Hook – handless horror of the oceans.

MARTIN (*looks nervously around him*). Sshh – don't! Be careful!

MURT. This ain't a good idea, Skylights.

SKYLIGHTS (*quickly – on edge*). His stare – like the bright blue of a November morning frozen into icicles – placed inside the very centre of each melancholy eye. He picks his victim – the blundering blubberous landlubber – known as Martin the Cabin Boy.

SKYLIGHTS *closes in on* MARTIN. *Behind him,* HOOK *enters.* HOOK *is an ageing cowboy, beaten chaps, a velvet waistcoat, frock coat, curls beneath a leather Stetson, spurred boots. You can tell he was incredible in his prime, but now – heavily tanned with yellow teeth – his thin lips pucker around his double cigar-holder. There is something of an ageing country star, a past-it boozer, a jaded cowboy.* HOOK's *bosun,* SMEE, *hangs at his side – tubby and shuffling, clearly enamoured with his captain.* SKYLIGHTS *confuses fear for rapture – he rolls on with added flare.*

MARTIN. N-n-no.

SKYLIGHTS. Y– y– yes – as little Martin tries to tie his shoes and fails cos 'is fingers is too fat – an evil rage begins to bubble in our cruel Captain – and quickly – then! Them blue eyes turn fiery red; his horrible hoof snaps out – ha! (*Mimics a throat being cut*). The insides of every buccaneer buckle as they see the throat ripped right out of him. And the Captain just kicks the body aside before his lapdog Smee comes to tenderly, carefully wipe the bloodied Hook with his own miserable little paw.

HOOK *laughs and claps slowly – tapping his hook against his belt buckle.* SKYLIGHTS *freezes at the sound.*

HOOK. Such a damned shame, Skylights.

SKYLIGHTS. C-c-captain, I –

HOOK. How many times – 'to tenderly, carefully wipe' – tell me what offends.

SKYLIGHTS. C-c-captain, I – I...

HOOK. Nothing aggravates me more than a split infinitive, Skylights, and what kind of Captain would I be if I let such misdemeanours go unpunished? Hm?

HOOK*'s hook appears over* SKYLIGHT*'s shoulder.*

SKYLIGHTS. Grammar's never been my –

HOOK *draws his hook across* SKYLIGHTS*' neck.* SKYLIGHTS *falls lifeless to the ground.*

SMEE. Oh, well done, Captain. Good show – lovely work, expert.

SMEE *wipes* HOOK*'s hook.*

HOOK. I wasn't aware it was story-time?

Pause. The PIRATES *freeze and look at* HOOK, *slightly confused by the question.*

You're meant to be finding Peter Pan. (*Booming, terrifying.*) Go!

The PIRATES *exit.*

SMEE. They'll boldly go, sir.

HOOK. Oh, Smee.

HOOK *slaps a confused* SMEE *across the face with his glove.* SMEE *smilingly takes it.*

(*Holding his cigar-holder out to* SMEE.) It's clogged with gunk.

SMEE *takes it and cleans it, lovingly.*

SMEE. My pleasure.

HOOK. It's almost dusk.

SMEE. Aye, Captain.

HOOK. We're not going to find him before dark, are we?

SMEE. The dogs are out looking.

HOOK. I want that boy dead – I want his head on a spike – I want his blood, Smee! And still we can't get him. Look at me!

SMEE. I'm always looking at you, Captain.

HOOK. My hair is starting to grey.

SMEE. I think it looks distinguished.

HOOK. I have a face like a dry chamois.

SMEE. You can mark the miles you've sailed, see the battles you've won – aye, sir, but that's nothing to be ashamed of, that's pride, etched in there. You hear?

HOOK. The soft light of evening, the gentle song of the starlings, look at those starlings, how they stare at me – with contempt, Smee – with pity!

HOOK *takes out a pistol and shoots*.

SMEE (*inspecting it*). That's a pine cone, sir.

HOOK. The pain of age, the endless ache of regret – and Pan is out there playing.

HOOK *lets out a guttural roar and stabs his dagger into a tree, then collapses defeated, tormented*.

The oboe, Smee, it's time for the oboe.

SMEE. No, sir – surely /

HOOK. / The oboe!

SMEE *rather begrudgingly gets out a retractable oboe from his shorts and begins to play a wistful melody in the minor key for* HOOK *to lament to*.

The sun is setting – the evening of my life draws in, oh, Smee, how cold it grows, how cold. Where now are the friends I once danced with in those long summers of my youth? Where now are the severed heads of my enemies? Where now is my ginormous booty?

SMEE *chokes a little on his oboe.*

I am but a collection of unfulfilled dreams, the empty husk of the promising corn of youth; chaff, Smee – chaff!

HOOK *spits and strikes a tragic pose.* SMEE *defiantly stops playing the oboe.*

SMEE. Come on, Captain, it's just the twilight – eh? It's making you monologue, it always does. We'll get you a G and T – pop in one of them lovely umbrellas you like, look – I've cleaned this right out – here we go –

SMEE *lights the cigars and puts the holder into* HOOK*'s mouth as if he were a baby.* HOOK *dashes the cigar-holder on the ground and leaps to his feet. He strides downstage and wields his sword at the audience – staring out into the dark.*

HOOK. Their disgusting little eyes sparkling in the dark – their horrid little faces grinning – I will kill every last child and feed them to the crocodile! Do you hear me, children? Go and find the crew, Smee, tell them we'll not sleep tonight. We won't rest until Pan is dead!

SMEE *exits.*

There! I can hear something in the trees. It's children, Smee – we've found them – Smee! Smee?

HOOK *dashes forward towards the forest – but suddenly freezes; from the forest comes the* CROCODILE *– half-reptile, half-doctor, the ticking clock to test for a pulse getting louder and louder.*

Come on… come on –

HOOK *holds fast, but the* CROCODILE *opens its jaws and* HOOK *falters – he can't stand it.*

HOOK *exits, pursued by* CROCODILE.

Scene Two

TOOTLES *appears, as if by magic, from a Never Tree – he's holding his bow and arrow out ready to shoot the* CROCODILE, *his eyes are scrunched.*

TOOTLES. I'm not afraid, I'm not afraid –

He can't quite bring himself to shoot – he opens his eyes and the CROCODILE *has gone.*

No! (*Throws his bow on the ground in frustration.*) I bet if I had a mother she could tell me, 'Tootles, my brave son, you are so brave,' she might say. I'm very tired, in my tummy, of not knowing.

TOOTLES *is about to slope off when* TINK*'s bright light lands on his shoulder.*

Tink? Tink! You're back! Where's Peter? A white bird? Where? Yes – I see it, Tink – I see it! I'll do it! I'm the one to do it!

TOOTLES *aims and shoots like a champion. The arrow hits* WENDY. WENDY *comes tumbling to the ground.*

I hit it! I am brave! I *am* brave! Boys! Boys!

TOOTLES *looks at* WENDY.

Tink? Tink, this doesn't look like a bird. Tink?

She's vanished from sight.

I think I may have made a – mistake.

We can hear the chatter of LOST BOYS *approaching from their trees.* TOOTLES *panics, and covers* WENDY *with leaves. The chatter suddenly stops – all is quiet.* TOOTLES *is scared. Then, suddenly – an ambush –* CURLY, NIBS *and* SLIGHTLY *come charging on, their weapons brandished. They scream,* TOOTLES *screams. They all scream until face to face they stop.*

NIBS. Tootles!

TOOTLES. What?

NIBS. We thought you were – real and present danger.

TOOTLES (*trying to conceal* WENDY *all the while*). Well, I'm not, I'm just Tootles.

CURLY (*heading toward* WENDY *to sit down*). I'm very glad you're not a pirate.

TOOTLES (*redirecting* CURLY). Don't sit there – there's, um – parrot poo.

NIBS (*starts sniffing the ground*). They must be close – there's sea-smoke coming in. (*Licks his finger and holds it up in the air.*)

CURLY *flumps on the ground.*

(*Desperately trying to lift* CURLY *up again, grunting with the effort.*) No – no – no sitting. We are on the verge of flinging ourselves into battle /

SLIGHTLY (*also sitting*). / My feet hurt.

NIBS. No!

TOOTLES. Nibs is right – we should move on – it's too open here and look the sun is slipping and oh look –

TOOTLES *blows air at the back of* NIBS*'s head.*

A tornado! Quick – we should go!

CURLY. What do you think, Slightly – is it nap time? Is it proper? It is, isn't it? A little crumpet and a snooze?

SLIGHTLY. One must only eat cake and take a nap at teatime and it isn't really the time for tea.

NIBS. It's the time for murder.

CURLY. Says who?

SLIGHTLY. The Queen. Mostly.

CURLY. Imagine that? You can make all the rules in the world and you decide on less cake. If you ask me, that is an

unforgivable waste of an opportunity, I have a mind to write
a strongly worded letter /

NIBS. / We are incredibly savage savages in very real and
present danger; we do not eat crumpets and take naps!

CURLY. If we had a mother, I bet she'd say it was nap time.

NIBS. Savages don't need mothers.

NIBS *tries to head towards* WENDY *in a huff and*
TOOTLES *stands in his way.*

CURLY. She'd make a huge soft bed with bundles of blankets
warmed by a little fire and /

SLIGHTLY. / Mother's beds aren't like our beds – when you've
been very good – she makes you an – apple-pie bed.

CURLY. Oh – oh my – oh my – that is – tell me more, tell me
everything.

NIBS. Out of my way, Tootles!

TOOTLES. Um, no – I – I think I saw the pirates go the other
way.

NIBS. We've just come from there.

SLIGHTLY. The pillow is made of pastry and you get to nibble
it before bed and when you climb in the mother comes and
sits by you and says it's time to tuck in!

CURLY (*swoons with pleasure*). Oh, listen, Nibs – please can
we get a mother? Please?

NIBS (*exploding*). I only get to be Captain when Peter is away
and Peter isn't away very much so I just think – all this not
doing what I say just isn't letting me be very captainy – is it?
Now, we are boys – savage savage wild ferocious boys and
we are hunting pirates, okay? So no naps, no cake, no
mothers and that – (*Suddenly spots the mound behind*
TOOTLES.) Tootles, what's that?

TOOTLES. What's what?

NIBS. That – behind you.

TOOTLES. A hillock. A white – snowy – hillock.

NIBS. Are you sure it's a hillock?

TOOTLES *wobbles and bursts into tears.*

TOOTLES. No, no, I'm not at all sure it's a hillock.

NIBS. Savages don't cry.

TOOTLES. I don't think I am a savage.

TOOTLES *steps aside and the* BOYS *uncover* WENDY – *stunned silence.*

NIBS. I think you might be.

TOOTLES. Tink said that Peter wanted us to shoot the white bird – s-so I shot it.

CURLY. Tootles?

TOOTLES. When Nibs hits a bird you all cheer but when I /

SLIGHTLY. / That's not a bird, Tootles.

CURLY. It's a lady.

TOOTLES. N-n-no it's not.

CURLY. Peter must have brought us a mother.

TOOTLES. No.

TOOTLES *falls to his knees besides* WENDY.

When ladies used to come to me in dreams, I would say 'Pretty Mother – I am so glad of you' – but when, at last, she really came… I shot her.

Beat. The LOST BOYS *look at* TOOTLES. PETER *appears. He is somersaulting and leaping around – he is especially full of beans, even for* PETER. *He lands. The* BOYS *look a little wary.* PETER *crows. The* BOYS *crow in response but it's a little weak.*

PETER. Nibs, what's the report? Any attacks? Have you spotted him? I saw the *Jolly Roger* in the south end of the lagoon as I flew over but it looks unmanned so they must be… (*Notices that they are all very silent.*) Something is funny.

The LOST BOYS *all laugh heartily.*

Not funny haha, funny strange.

The LOST BOYS *try to do funny strange.*

Not that kind of funny either.

The LOST BOYS *all get stuck trying to be neither funny or strange.* PETER *looks at them sideways.*

(*Suddenly joyous.*) You know, don't you? You've seen her, the Wendy – already – that's why! Yes – I brought you a mother. She's great, isn't she? That thing she does with her face – right? Right?

The BOYS *part,* TOOTLES *takes* PETER*'s hand and leads him to* WENDY*'s body.*

Oh. She's dead.

TOOTLES. Yes.

Pause.

PETER. Let's go.

CURLY. What?

PETER. To the lagoon, pick up your weapons!

NIBS *and* PETER *head off,* CURLY *and* SLIGHTLY *loiter, a little unsure, and* TOOTLES *stands resolutely by* WENDY.

TOOTLES. But, Peter, we should be sad and sorry.

PETER. What's the point in that?

Beat. The BOYS *don't have an answer.*

Well then.

PETER *spots an arrow on the floor next to* WENDY.

An arrow? A Lost Boy arrow. Who shot this?

TOOTLES. Me.

PETER. You shot the Wendy?

PETER *is ready to plunge the arrow into* TOOTLES*'s chest – who is very brave about the whole thing – when* WENDY *rouses.*

WENDY. No.

NIBS. No? Someone said /

CURLY. / She did.

PETER. Hello, Wendy.

WENDY. It didn't hit me – it hit the... hello, Peter.

PETER. It hit my kiss – my kiss saved your life! My kiss saved her life!

WENDY. Well, yes – I guess, you could say that.

CURLY. Slightly, what's a kiss?

WENDY. Are these the lost boys?

PETER. Yes. Yes! And this is Neverland and – and – you're alive!

SLIGHTLY *looks at the button around* WENDY*'s neck.*

SLIGHTLY. Yes, I remember, quite well now – I could do kisses very well from a young age. I used to kiss my trousers before I went to school.

TOOTLES (*stepping away and being proper*). Hello, Wendy; we are the Lost Boys and Peter is our Captain.

NIBS. I am Second Captain, Nibs.

PETER. Nibs is quick and brave, like me but a bit less.

CURLY. I am Curly – and I'm –

CURLY *gets overwhelmed and just gives* WENDY *a huge hug.*

SLIGHTLY. I'm affrighted to cake your acquaintance.

SLIGHTLY *half-bows, half-curtsies.* CURLY *puts* WENDY *down, a little embarrassed.*

CURLY. Slightly remembers the most of the ways of the grown-ups; the proper ways – sorry for squeezing so hard.

WENDY (*gives* CURLY *a squeeze*). It's okay.

SLIGHTLY. I am Slightly, Slightly Soiled. You see I'm from the
Soiled Family – it said so on my tag when I arrived – so as I
am the only proper gentleman, I should like to shake hands.

*SLIGHTLY shakes his hand at WENDY, sort of waggles it
in her face.*

WENDY. It's like this. And you say 'How do you do?'

*WENDY takes SLIGHTLY's hand and shakes it properly.
SLIGHTLY looks a little concerned that he's been rumbled.*

SLIGHTLY. Yes, of course. I remember now.

The BOYS break into a round of 'How do you do's.

WENDY. And this is?

PETER. Tootles. He's the youngest, he –

TOOTLES. Will protect you if you ever need it – or if you are
afraid of the dark – then I'm a good person to talk to.

The BOYS all laugh a bit but TOOTLES keeps his chin up.

WENDY. Well, it's really lovely to meet you all. Is this all of
you?

SLIGHTLY. Are we not enough?

CURLY. I can try to be two.

CURLY tries to be two.

WENDY. No – you are – you're wonderful. It's just that I'm
here to find another lost boy – he's called Tom and he's
about this tall and he's got blue eyes and brown hair and /

NIBS. / Another Lost Boy? But there aren't any other /

PETER. / Wait till you see our Home Under the Ground – it's
amazing, there are glow-worms and bunk beds and – and –
tonight! We'll have a feast and I'll play my pipes and we can
dance and /

WENDY. / But I need to go and /

CURLY. / You can't leave – you're our mother.

WENDY (*laughs*). Your mother?

TOOTLES. Yes.

WENDY. You don't have a mother?

SLIGHTLY. We will have little arguments that may seem awful at the time but in the long run will only serve to develop character and bring us closer together.

WENDY. I can't be a mother, I'm only a girl – I –

WENDY *looks at the* LOST BOYS. SLIGHTLY, CURLY *and* TOOTLES *have crowded around her, their faces raised and eyelids fluttering and big grins, it is impossibly persuasive.* NIBS *stands a little way off, wary, and* PETER *hangs right back, sultry and playing something bluesy on his pipes – he is equally persuasive.*

PETER. Please, Wendy – we'd love you to stay and darn socks and make breakfast and tell stories and /

TOOTLES. / Give us medicine.

CURLY. And tell us to tuck in!

WENDY. But, Peter, I have to look for –

PETER. Don't go.

WENDY. But there is only one of me and all these boys and I'm not sure I could be Mother or if I'd have the time because I should really be looking for /

PETER. / I could help you. Um – I could –

WENDY. Be Father?

PETER. I could play Father. Will you stay?

WENDY. Well yes – of course.

WENDY *moves toward* PETER *to give him a celebratory hug and* PETER *steps away, not wanting to be touched. The* LOST BOYS *cheer and dance about – leaving* WENDY *and* PETER *standing looking at one another, a slight tension hanging between them.* MICHAEL *and* JOHN *come running in from the undergrowth, looking like they've really been*

through it – leaves in their hair, mud on their faces. JOHN
looks at all the hugging and is appalled.

JOHN. Good Lord, what on earth is going on here – this is not
cricket.

WENDY. John! Michael! You're here – look! These are the
Lost Boys! Aren't they wonderful!

JOHN. Wendy – step away – let's all just calm down, shall we?

MICHAEL *charges right on over and leaps into the group
hug.*

MICHAEL. How lovely!

JOHN. Michael – get a hold of yourself! I mean – just stop,
everyone, stop getting a hold of everyone!

MICHAEL. Wendy – you won't believe how many rare plants
and flowers there are! There are jungles that go on and on –
and flowers that crawl and singing flamingos and rivers with
multicoloured bubbles and mermaids – a whole lagoon of
mermaids! It's just like I dreamt it! It's amazing!

WENDY *squeezes* MICHAEL *tight.* CURLY, TOOTLES
and SLIGHTLY *grab* JOHN *and* MICHAEL *and start
leading them into the Home Under the Ground.*

CURLY. To the Home Under the Ground!

PETER *crows.*

WENDY *catches* PETER *just before he goes – they are the
only ones left above ground.*

WENDY. Hey – wait, um /

PETER. / Hm?

WENDY. I'm very glad you fell through my window.

PETER *starts pretending to be a monkey and dancing
round* WENDY, *picking through her hair, 'oo-oo' ing.*
WENDY *laughs, starts pretending to be a monkey as well.
They both get the giggles –* WENDY *suddenly stops and
looks at* PETER.

Are you glad to be Father?

PETER. One girl is worth more than a thousand boys.

WENDY. Oh.

> WENDY *turns away, coy. When she turns back* – PETER *is gone*.

> Wait – there's someone there. Peter! Peter! I need to see if it's...

> WENDY *crouches low and hides herself in the undergrowth; she sees something moving through the hedges. She watches.*

Scene Three

WENDY *crouches, hidden in the clearing – a hooded figure is shooting arrows,* WENDY *approaches with caution.*

WENDY. Tom?

> *The figure turns to* WENDY.

> Oh, it is – oh, at last I –

> *The figure raises an arrow at* WENDY.

> I – I'm sorry – I – thought you were someone else. Please don't shoot. I've already been shot once today and I'm – quite tired.

> *The figure lowers its bow and turns to go.*

> Thank you. Thank you.

> *Beat – the figure walks away.*

> Who are you?

> *The figure snaps round and raises its bow again.*

> Are you a – pirate?

TIGER LILY *raises her bow at* WENDY.

> I'll take that as a no. You're not a Lost Boy /

TIGER LILY. / How could you tell?

WENDY. Look, if you're going to shoot me just get on and do it and if you aren't then have the manners to stop pointing that thing at me.

TIGER LILY *drops the arrow and drops the hood of the cape. She's wearing a hoody with jeans, hi-tops, her hair is braided. She's young, early teens, black with a vibe of impossible cool, she has the look of someone ready to move. She has a hand-axe slung through her belt and an amazing bow and quiver slung across her body with 'Tiger' etched on the side.*

TIGER LILY. Wow – kid's got courage. Now scram – it's not safe out here.

WENDY. No – I'm – I'm looking for a Lost Boy – he's about this tall with a big smile – he's six – wait, no – he'd be seven by now – and I think he's in the forest /

TIGER LILY. / All the Lost Boys live with Pan. Now I got to go.

WENDY. No, look – wait – the boy I lost was my brother; I need to get him back… I need to fix my family.

TIGER LILY *stops and turns back to* WENDY *– something has moved her, changed her. She nods hello.*

TIGER LILY. Tiger Lily.

WENDY. I'm Wendy.

TIGER LILY. I'm sorry but I haven't seen your brother.

WENDY. Could you help us look?

TIGER LILY. I got a mission of my own. I'm sorry.

WENDY. But if you're not a Lost Boy or a pirate or a fairy then, what – what are you?

TIGER LILY. I had a tribe; we were the Picins.

WENDY. What happened?

TIGER LILY. Captain Hook happened. Just like I'm going to happen to Captain Hook when I get him. So /

WENDY. / So you're not part of /

TIGER LILY. / I'm part of me. /

WENDY. / Well then you have to come and join us – there is plenty of room and the boys are so warm and welcoming and /

TIGER LILY. / I said – I'm part of me.

WENDY. You don't have to be lonely.

TIGER LILY. I'm alone – there's a difference. Shhh! You hear that? They're close – they're on the wind. Go – go now, get back underground or they'll have you.

WENDY. But you don't have a father or a husband or brothers or – who looks after you?

> TIGER LILY *turns to go and* WENDY *steps in her way, she's transfixed, captivated.*

Can I hold it? Your – bow – can I?

Beat.

> TIGER LILY *looks about nervously then hands the bow over.*

TIGER LILY. Easy, she's tricky – and be quick.

> WENDY *holds the bow – holds it up, as if it's magic. The power of it is hugely exciting to her.*

WENDY. It feels… amazing.

> TIGER LILY *goes to take the bow back off* WENDY. WENDY *holds onto it for a moment.*

Please help me.

TIGER LILY. You ever wondered why there ain't no lost girls?

WENDY. Peter said that girls are too smart to fall out their prams.

TIGER LILY (*laughs*). They got tired of taking orders, patchin' knees – they wanted to play things their way. They left. They're there though –

WENDY. In the forest?

TIGER LILY takes WENDY by the hand and leads her to the edge of the stage – they stare out at all the little girls.

TIGER LILY. Sometimes – when it's dead quiet and you look real hard, you can sense 'em – out there, ready – all them girls, ready for their big adventure – just waiting for their moment, hm?

The eerie sound of the pirate horn calls out across the forest. TIGER LILY jumps.

Go, now – that's the sea-dog call – they're hunting again – they're coming this way. Get underground /

WENDY. / I'll come, I'll help you – I'll get the boys.

TIGER LILY. No! You give Pan my victory and I'll kill you.

WENDY. He promised – he said he'd help – he /

TIGER LILY. / Peter Pan don't take no orders off no one – you want to find your brother – you're going to need to go solo.

TIGER LILY draws an arrow and sets it up – and heads into the forest. WENDY stands, stubborn.

WENDY (*shouting after her*). 'When you act like a lady it brings out the gentlemen in men'!

TIGER LILY stops short, shakes her head – turns to WENDY.

TIGER LILY. How come they don't never have to grow up but you got to be playing Mother from the get-go? It don't seem fair to me.

TIGER LILY exits into the forest. WENDY stands, furious. The sea-dog call comes again – WENDY is suddenly scared, alone – she walks back the way she came and unwittingly falls through one of the entrances into the Home Under the Ground. We follow her down, down into the magical lair.

Scene Four

*The Home Under the Ground is the world underneath your bed,
at first dark and mysterious but soon a treasure trove of
adventure. As* WENDY *flies in, it is already alive with magical,
joyful activity.* PETER *plays his harmonica, making the flames
from the fire dance up along the walls.* TINK *sits up in her
room overseeing the action – the* BOYS *busy around beneath.*

WENDY. It's okay – it's all right – I'm here and I'm okay – you
can stop…

   WENDY *looks up and sees all the* BOYS *thoroughly
   engrossed in what they're doing.*

   …worrying. (*Captivated for a moment.*) Wow.

   WENDY *goes over to* PETER.

   Oh, Peter – there you are – um – I –

PETER. Hello.

WENDY. Hi.

PETER. Biscuit face.

WENDY. Oh – thanks, I know but um –

MICHAEL. Hey – Wendy! You're here, isn't it amazing!

WENDY. Well – yes – it is – just, Peter, do you think we might
make a plan – to find Tom?

PETER. You don't really plan adventures, you just /

WENDY. / Maybe we could plan this one, though? Maybe?

PETER. Three hundred and twenty-eight pirates – never had a
plan.

WENDY. Okay – well, as Mother I say we have to make a plan.

PETER. But it's playtime.

WENDY. It's plantime.

PETER. But I'm Father – and I say we can't make a plan unless
I say so.

WENDY. As Mother – I tell you, Father – to say that we *are*
going to make a plan.

PETER. I haven't had any pie.

WENDY. What?

PETER. Slightly says that when a mother wants a father to do
something that he doesn't want to do, she cooks a pie.

WENDY. No, Peter, that's not quite right that's /

PETER. / That's what Slightly said and if Slightly said it then –

PETER *leaps off to something new.* WENDY *turns, furious,
and strides over to* SLIGHTLY. SLIGHTLY *is bent over with
his head down a fishing hole.*

WENDY. Slightly? Slightly!

SLIGHTLY. Sorry, Wendy – I'm a bit – busy – I –

WENDY. Slightly, will you please tell Peter that /

CURLY. / Mother! There is a hole in my sock!

WENDY. Yes – one minute.

SLIGHTLY *pulls his head out of the hole – he's wielding
two sticks.*

SLIGHTLY. How can I be of help to you, Mother?

WENDY *winces, her hand to her nose and backs off.*

WENDY. What is that?

SLIGHTLY. Do you want to play? I'm playing poo sticks.

WENDY. Slightly, that's not what Pooh Sticks is – oh, oh –

SLIGHTLY *disappears back down the hole.*

Peter! Peter!

WENDY *turns back and sees* PETER *playing and laughing
with* TINK. *She feels too threatened to get involved. She
spots* MICHAEL *in his botanical laboratory, who is
explaining something very smart to* TOOTLES.

Michael – Michael? Do you know what they're laughing about /

MICHAEL. / If we take this flower of division magnoliophyta and we add its nectar to the glow-worm compound /

WENDY. / Michael /

MICHAEL. / One moment, Wendy – this is very precise work /

WENDY. / No – look, there's no time for games – I need, we have to find /

MICHAEL. / Um – games? Actually – I think you'll find that this is incredibly important botanical research /

TOOTLES. / Michael – should I keep adding?

WENDY picks up a flower.

WENDY. Oh, look! This flower is sneezing!

MICHAEL. No – a – please don't touch – (*Grabs the flower back from* WENDY.) Contamination! They're very delicate and chubby girl fingers are not –

WENDY picks up a lantern with a fairy in the bottom of it.

TOOTLES. How much is enough?

WENDY. It's a fairy!

MICHAEL. She's under controlled conditions.

WENDY. She's drunk and smoking a pipe.

TOOTLES. Michael, it's getting a bit bubbly.

MICHAEL. Give it back.

WENDY. Not until you promise to help me find Tom.

The experiment that TOOTLES *is looking after explodes everywhere.*

MICHAEL. It's ruined!

WENDY. Michael – listen to me.

MICHAEL. I'll never get the Nobel Prize now.

WENDY. Michael!

MICHAEL. All my work!

WENDY. Oh, for Pete's sake –

PETER. Me?

WENDY. No – no – but actually, yes, Peter – look, please come down here.

PETER moves as if to go down – TINK makes a big 'under the thumb' action.

TINK. Under the thumb? What?

PETER scowls at her and stays where he is.

CURLY. Mother, what does it mean when my tummy is rumbling and it hurts a bit?

WENDY. Oh, Curly, I'm sorry – it means – it means I should make breakfast.

The mere sound of the word 'breakfast' and the whole room – without looking up – erupts into 'toast', 'one eggs over-easy', 'coffee', 'no sugar', etc.

I'll do it in just a second – just, Peter, can you stop playing a moment – and /

TINK. / I thought making sure her kids was fed was top of the list for a good mother?

WENDY (*red-faced and furious*). Why don't you try and be Mother, hm?

TINK. I'm sorry – I didn't hear that – do come a bit closer.

WENDY marches towards TINK, one foot disappears down a fishing hole, TINK finds it hilarious.

Oop, careful – fishing hole!

WENDY is furious. She pulls her wet foot out of the hole and leans on a rock – she burns her hand.

Ooh – easy there – firefly!

TINK *bursts into laughter once more*.

Cor, wreck and ruin – I reckon Mum's been on the gin again.

WENDY. I thought you were only big when you were full of feeling? You seem to be rather large all the time.

TINK. You got a bit a pondweed on your face, babe.

WENDY. Ugh!

TINK. Delighted – by the way – I'm brim-full of bleedin' delighted!

TINK *grins at* WENDY.

Another tug at WENDY*'s dress.*

CURLY. You look a bit angry, Mother, does cooking breakfast with me and being in the home with your children make you angry?

WENDY. It's quite hard to find Tom, be Mother and have fun all at the same time!

JOHN. Any news on that breakfast, Wendy?

WENDY. Right – breakfast – make breakfast, be fun and find... Curly – let's make breakfast!

CURLY. I been trying see – (*Lifts up a dubious-looking saucepan.*) Worms and custard – but I think it curdled, which is odd because custard is usually my specialty.

WENDY *looks and nearly gags.*

WENDY. How about we make some bacon – just – as well – just – in case.

CURLY. Oh yes! Oh yes! Lovely! Oh, Mother – you are the best! I am so – so glad of you!

CURLY *picks* WENDY *up and spins her round.* WENDY *finally seems a little happy, and gets in the spirit – just enough to suggest.*

WENDY. Maybe we could even make a game of bacon?

CURLY *drops* WENDY *immediately and looks very grave.*

CURLY. No, bacon is serious, very seriously yummy and I don't think anyone should make a game of it... not even mothers.

WENDY. Oh. Right.

CURLY storms off, dropping his custard pot all over the floor.

Oh, Curly – the custard – who's going to clear it up? The fairies?

TINK. Fat chance.

WENDY. I was being sarcastic.

TINK. Don't use your fancy words with me.

WENDY. Will somebody please just stop and listen to me!

WENDY steps back onto the plans for the Shimminy Flip.

JOHN. Wendy!

WENDY. Oh, John – at last, thank you – look, if you could just get everyone together in one place then I've got a plan for us to –

JOHN puts his oily hand over WENDY's face to stop her talking – WENDY tries to mumble through it.

JOHN. Shh – shh – Okay, Nibs – few more twondles and the little beauty'll be ready to ruckle! We just need to – uh –

NIBS. You want to be getting the shaft crank attached firmly to the, uh –

JOHN. Ratchet plank – use a sprogget or a shifty – got a pair of plonders in the box.

NIBS. Yeah yeah yeah yeah yeah.

WENDY escapes from the hand. She goes to pick up the plonders, keen to be helpful.

JOHN. Oooh. No. Never mind.

WENDY looks deflated. JOHN turns back to play.

WENDY. John!

JOHN. Stay back, Wendy, wouldn't want you to get oil on your, you – know – that. (*Points to her nightie.*)

WENDY. John, I want you to listen to me.

JOHN. Something's whining – there's a – (*Imitates.*)

NIBS. Yeah – what is that? Ooh it's horrible.

JOHN. It's probably the sprinkets round the histon runge.

NIBS. Yeah yeah yeah yeah. Pass the crook notch.

JOHN. Yuh, yuh, yuh, yuh – hoofty it on seamless to the splocket, tightening up the trundle as you go and –

WENDY. John Darling! I said – listen to me!

JOHN. That whine… it's getting worse. I'd give it a quick sploosh sploosh with the noodle cleaner –

NIBS. Oop – there you go!

The machine bursts into life and with a chug throws WENDY *back on her bum.*

JOHN. Safe as houses, Bob's your dobber.

NIBS. Sroggedy do!

NIBS *and* JOHN *slap one another heartily on the back, shake hands.* WENDY *just about stumbles to her feet – takes a breath to scream,* PETER *spins her round and round with fairy dust.*

PETER. You need to unwind.

WENDY. There's a lot to remember – there's breakfast and who likes what and the hole in Curly's sock and no one has had their medicine yet and –

PETER. Just play!

WENDY. But you asked me to be Mother.

PETER *sprinkles and pulls out a bunch of flowers.*

PETER. Madam!

WENDY. But I'm really rather tired, Peter, would you make me a cup of tea?

PETER *sprinkles fairy dust on the wall and pulls out a stretchy slug.*

PETER. Stretchy slug!

WENDY. Look – you asked me to be Mother and said you'd be Father so it's your responsibility to help me.

PETER *freezes at the word 'responsibility' – picks up two teddies and tries to entertain* WENDY *with them.*

Not having a plan is actually just following your plan not to have a plan! And it's mean because by making your plan no plan – it makes anyone that wants to do anything different seem all cross and grumpy and –

PETER *looks terrified, a little bit queasy. He brandishes the teddy bears at* WENDY, *pushing their faces together like they are kissing.* WENDY *looks alarmed/questioning.* PETER, *suddenly aware, gets overwhelmed and awkward and makes the teddies kill one another.* WENDY *doesn't know what to do.* PETER *throws the teddies on the floor. Weird beat where they stare at one another, it's all a bit Freudian.* PETER *leaps off.*

He's completely mental.

WENDY *dashes off after him.*

Haven't you ever had a mother, Peter? Don't you remember how lovely it is to be quiet and listen to her read stories, to let her tuck you in and sing songs and give you medicine – Peter? To let her make a plan for the day – don't you remember?

PETER *looks at* WENDY *a moment.* WENDY *goes to touch him –* PETER *leaps away, as if he's fighting something, then suddenly:*

PETER. Bubble ball – let's set up the pitch! Bubble baaaaalll!

WENDY. Could someone explain the rules?

NIBS. You'll pick it up as you go along!

The BOYS *all cheer and the pitch is set up. It's all a crazy muddle.* WENDY *has no idea what's going on, she's dashing here and there and can't understand. The game*

*starts getting played around her. The game is fast-paced
and exciting and strangely similar to football. The ball
passes from team to team.* JOHN *is doing really well, his
feet start to lift off the floor.*

JOHN. Ah-ha! Look! Look!

WENDY. John?

NIBS. He's flying.

PETER. John has found his happy thought!

WENDY. John, what colour are Mother's eyes?

JOHN. Brown.

WENDY. They're blue. What does Father do for a living?

CURLY. Go, John, go!

WENDY. Michael?

MICHAEL. Father's a pirate.

WENDY. No, he's a lawyer! How many Darling children are
there, John? John?

JOHN. Three!! Michael, John and Wendy!

WENDY. No – you're wrong – we lost a boy!

JOHN *comes crashing down to the floor with a thud, furious,
the* LOST BOYS *stop.*

JOHN. You're always ruining all the fun!

WENDY. No – I – John, I'm sorry – I /

JOHN. / Leave me alone!

JOHN *storms out. Long pause. The* BOYS *stand in silence.*

WENDY. I don't want to be un-fun. I – it's just – if I don't
remember, then who… (*Pause.*) I didn't sew his button on. I
played battles instead and he got cold. It's my fault. It's my
fault we lost him.

The BOYS *look blankly at her – dumbfounded by the
outburst.*

MICHAEL. Wendy, you're clearly overtired, perhaps you should have a lie-down.

WENDY. Bog off, Michael. I have to find him. I'm going to find him – and I will be Captain.

TOOTLES. But Peter is Captain.

WENDY. Well – maybe – just for once… (*Standing up on a chair.*) I am Wendy Darling, I am brave and strong and – and I am going on an adventure! Who's with me?

The LOST BOYS *slope over to* PETER*'s side and then slope off to bed.*

CURLY. Oh, I don't like it when Mother gets shouty.

WENDY. Michael?

MICHAEL *walks away.*

MICHAEL. You're a damsel.

WENDY. Tootles?

TOOTLES. I can't imagine getting cuddles from a pirate fighter.

MICHAEL. Please don't go, wait for Peter or John or –

WENDY (*stepping down*). Okay fine, fine, that's it – fine – I'll do it by myself.

WENDY *storms away to go and pack her things into a bag. The rest of the* LOST BOYS *retreat, but* PETER *keeps trying.* MRS DARLING *enters – she is holding a suitcase and preparing to leave the house, she has defiance in her face.* MR DARLING *enters.*

MR DARLING. Where are you going?

PETER. Wendy?

MRS DARLING. You've been out all night. Where have you been?

WENDY. Why won't you help me?

MR DARLING. It's not enough to stay at home and look after your children.

PETER. You can't leave – you're Mother.

MRS DARLING. There's breakfast on the table.

WENDY. I can't, not on my own, and play games and find Tom and find my happy thought and – I can't.

MR DARLING. You will not leave this house – it is your duty –

PETER. Why don't you stay and we can play and –

MRS DARLING. To suggest I have been held in this house by duty is to deny fifteen years of affection and common understanding, if you keep me here, now – by duty – you may win a wife in name and function but you will lose everything that we hold dear.

WENDY. I thought you… you gave me a – (*Looks at the button around her neck.*) button.

MR DARLING. I will not be seen to have you work /

PETER. / Wendy?

MRS DARLING. We lost our boy, how can you still give a damn about losing face?

WENDY *and* MRS DARLING *pick up their suitcases and exit.* MR DARLING *and* PETER *look at one another for a moment – they seem to see something they recognise.*

MR DARLING *exits.*

PETER *stands, torn between going after* WENDY *and staying.* PETER *picks up his harmonica and tries to play a tune but thrashes it down in frustration.* PETER *chews his finger.* PETER *laughs.*

PETER. Will someone show me how to play Father because I don't think I know how… and there's nothing I don't know how to do. (*Stands ready to go to the door to go after her.*) I should go and get her… (*Sits defeated.*) but…

TINK. All right?

PETER. Tink – I didn't know you were still /

TINK. / Watching the rain and writing in your diary, mate?

PETER. No. Not – just – w-what do I do? I can't tell her, I can't
help her find her brother – because /

TINK. / Because looking for him is only going to make him
stay away longer.

PETER. But I can't tell her that because telling someone to try
and forget –

TINK. Only makes them remember twice as hard. I did warn ya.

PETER. Yes, all right.

TINK. Pete, you ain't a moper, you're a fighter. This girl – look,
she's got you all of a muddle and Peter Pan don't get in a
muddle. I don't like it, mate – it ain't you.

PETER. But Tink – she's /

TINK. / I wasn't going to mention it but – I 'eard a rumour.

PETER. What do mean a rumour? About me?

TINK. Fairy grapevine report is – Hook said: 'If only I'd
known that all it took to defeat Pan was some dipstick in a
nightie – what a wimp.'

PETER. Defeat? What? He hasn't defeated anything.

TINK. Well, mate – I'm just sayin'.

PETER. Get me my sword. Wake the Lost Boys; tell them to
meet me at Marooner's Rock.

TINK. I'm on it – all over it – oh, but – um – what about Wendy?

PETER. He's going to die this time. He's going to die!

PETER *exits*.

TINK. That's my boy. (*Aside*.) Oh, come on, it was only a
smidgy little white lie. (*Booming*.) Laaaaads! Up and at 'em
– we're going inta battle!

Scene Five

In the clearing above ground, WENDY *heads bravely through the woods, her knapsack in hand.*

WENDY. Oh, please don't get dark, not now. Come on, Wendy
– come on.

A twig cracks, the leaves ruffle.

What was that? Who's there?

She takes a few deep breaths. An arrow shoots up and over WENDY's *head; she cowers on the floor, the arrow pings into a tree next to her.* WENDY *looks and sees 'Tiger' written on the side.*

Tiger? Tiger Lily! Tiger Lily – it's Wendy! I'm sorry about before I was wrong /

TIGER LILY. / Wendy! Run!

WENDY *looks behind her – and too late – over her shoulder comes the savage claw of* HOOK. *He holds the metal to her neck and scoops her up in his spare arm.* SMEE *hurries to his side.* TIGER LILY *escapes.*

HOOK. Oh, looky looky, what have we here?

SMEE. It's a toucan.

HOOK. Troublingly large.

SMEE. A troublingly large toucan, Captain?

HOOK. But it's all alone.

SMEE. A one-can! That's it, a troublingly large one-can. Let's kill it.

WENDY. I'm not a one-can – I'm a girl.

HOOK *looks at her a moment.* HOOK *and* SMEE *look at one another, confused.*

HOOK. A what?

WENDY. A girl.

SMEE. A what?

WENDY. A small woman.

HOOK (*laughing riotously*). Oh, good God, Smee. It's been so long since I've seen one; I forgot how silly they look. Look at them – oh, look, ah – (*Crying with laughter, can barely contain himself.*) Ooh – look, their funny little hands and silly faces – ohh, ooof. Right, Hook, come on, pull yourself together. (*Raises his hook ready to bring it down.*)

WENDY (*screaming*). Peter! Peeeeeeter!

HOOK. Did you say... Peter?

WENDY (*quietly*). He'll save me. I know he will.

HOOK. Good Lord, Smee – I do believe that Peter Pan has gone and got himself a – mother!

HOOK laughs heartily, SMEE joins in – not really understanding why or what he's laughing at.

SMEE. What's a mother again?

HOOK. A mother, Smee – to wipe his nose and tie his shoelaces, to tuck him in and pat his head. Pathetic little Peter Pan needs a mother!

WENDY. I'm not his mother. I am Mother and he is Father.

Pause, HOOK stumbles slightly, genuinely shocked, as if it were grief.

HOOK. P-p-peter Pan? Father?

SMEE. Captain?

HOOK steps back, hides his face a moment.

HOOK (*gravely*). It's not possible. He can't... (*Beat.*) Where is he?

WENDY shakes her head.

(*Holds his hook to her neck.*) I said – tell us where he is.

WENDY shakes her head.

You'd risk your own neck to save that impudent boy?

WENDY (*looks at her feet, a little sad*). Yes.

HOOK (*furious*). Bind her, Smee!

> SMEE *sets to work on tying* WENDY *up*.

> (*Far downstage, out to audience.*) Pan, come, little sparrow, come and fight Captain Hook. Your youth is mine to extinguish – I will not have you give it up before I've had my fight. Do you hear me?!

> *From nowhere, an arrow strikes* HOOK *and he staggers backwards, for a moment we think he has been hit.*

> No, no! Bad form! Bad form!

SMEE. It's not got you – up – up – we're under attack!

HOOK. Smee, hold her! (*Raises his sword and bellows.*) Come on then!

> TIGER LILY *comes charging into battle.* HOOK *stands to receive her;* SMEE *and* WENDY *crouch behind him.*

WENDY. Tiger Lily!

HOOK. It's that damned Picin Princess!

SMEE. Oh oh.

HOOK. You said she was dead! You said you killed *all* the Picin tribe.

SMEE. Must a missed one?

HOOK. 'Missed one' – she's the blinking princess!

> TIGER LILY *charges in and clashes with* HOOK. *The fighting is impressive.*

TIGER LILY (*holds* HOOK *at sword's length*). You laughed when you put your sword through my father.

HOOK. How terribly impolite of me.

TIGER LILY. Not laughing now? Are we?

> TIGER LILY *and* HOOK *clash –* HOOK *pushes* TIGER LILY *back.* SMEE *dashes out,* WENDY *trips him up.*

WENDY. Now, Tiger Lily – now!

    PETER *lands and crows*.

    Peter! Peter!

TIGER LILY. No!

HOOK. Oh, how lovely to see you, old friend.

    HOOK *draws his sword on* PETER, PETER *draws his on* HOOK, *it's almost lusty*.

PETER. You crinkly-faced, limp-limbed, sad sack of a one-handed cabin boy.

HOOK. Not the hand, Peter – you know how I feel about the hand.

PETER. Back off, Tiger Lily.

WENDY. Help me, Peter! Tiger Lily, I'm over here!

TIGER LILY. You gunna whine us to death on them nasty-ass pipes?

HOOK. Now, now, children.

PETER. I'm actually pretty amazing at the harmonica, the boys say so.

HOOK. The danger of a loyal crew, Peter.

TIGER LILY. And what right you reckon you got to play the blues anyway, joy boy? You got no soul, got no fire behind the eyes – ting like vengeance is wasted on a boy that can't do nothing but play games.

HOOK. Bravo, Tiger – bravo.

    PETER *lets out an ungodly roar – and charges at* HOOK. *They clash, it's savage – it's wild.* HOOK *bites* PETER, PETER *scratches* HOOK. *It's feral.* TIGER LILY *enters the fray.* PETER *turns and runs his sword through* TIGER LILY *– she staggers and falls*.

WENDY. Peter, how could you?

    TIGER LILY *lies, lifeless on the ground.* SMEE *blows a whistle in his top pocket and* JONES *and* MURT *appear*.

SMEE. We got a prisoner. Take her back to the ship – keep her in the hold.

MURT. We passed the croc, sir – it's not far off!

HOOK. What?

JONES. We only outran it by a smidge.

SMEE. We got to go, Captain, now – now!

HOOK. Wait!

SMEE. Captain, it's getting close.

> SMEE *puts his hand over* WENDY*'s mouth.* MURT *and* JONES *exit, taking* TIGER LILY *with them.* PETER, *without a second thought for* TIGER LILY, *returns to* HOOK *– his dagger raised and real fire in his eyes. We see* PETER *as never before and* HOOK *suddenly seems in his prime.* HOOK *uses both his sword and his hook dexterously; it's electric.* PETER *gets his dagger up to* HOOK*'s throat. It's close – one more slip and* HOOK *is history.*

> Touch him and I'll kill her!

HOOK. No one ever went down in history for saving a lady.

WENDY. Peter, please – look at my biscuit face.

> PETER *decides to fight* HOOK. HOOK *gets the upper hand.* SMEE *sees that* HOOK *is safe.*

> Peter!

SMEE. Captain – the crocodile – Captain!

HOOK. Leave us, go!

> SMEE *drags* WENDY *away.* WENDY, *offstage, screams.* PETER *hears the scream and falters –* HOOK *stabs* PETER. *The* CROCODILE *nears.* HOOK *exits, pursued by* CROCODILE.

PETER. It is only a game. It is only a game... to die will be an awfully big adventure.

Interval.

ACT THREE

Scene One

The LOST BOYS *with* MICHAEL *and* JOHN *stand crowded around the body of* PETER, *their heads are bowed, sniffing can be heard.* TINK *stands in elaborate mourning dress.*

TINK. It were 'eartbreaking – best fight I've ever seen him fight – so – blinkin' – brave. And final moment, before he went – last thing he said: 'Take me to the Lost Boys – have 'em lean in real close and whisper their biggest wish and I'll take it with me and make it true' – go on, boys – on you go.

TINK turns away and can barely conceal a grin. The BOYS *all lean in at the same time, bending their heads down to* PETER.

PETER (*leaps up*). Ra!

The LOST BOYS *jump out their skin.* TINK *and* PETER *roll around laughing and high-five.* PETER *suddenly realises the* BOYS *have turned on him.*

Oh, come on – it was funny. No?

The BOYS *start chasing after* PETER *and* TINK. PETER *and* TINK *peg it – round and round – it becomes hysterical, joyous. The cloud of laughing* BOYS *dissipates and exits to reveal* MR DARLING *in his hat and coat desperately searching for his wife. He runs after the noise of the children, thinking he's seen her.*

MR DARLING. Mary? Mary?

One of the children has dropped a newspaper. MR DARLING *slumps on the pavement, alone. He picks up the paper, opens it out, the headline reads 'Women Gone Mad! Suffragettes Steal Wives! Pankhurst Fights Parliament!'* MR DARLING *scrunches the paper in red-faced alarm.*

No?

The children dash on again – this time headed up by TINK *who is hollering.* MR DARLING *is terrified, chased offstage by the bellowing woman and her crowd, to reveal…*

WENDY *tied and bound. She's desperately trying to wriggle out of her ropes but with little luck.* WENDY *gives up and looks sadly up at the stars.* MRS DARLING *appears, suitcase in hand – also looking up at the sky.*

WENDY. If I can see the stars here and Mum can see the stars at home then we must be under the same sky. Mother, if you can hear me… I really want to find Tom but – but I'm – I'm scared. (*Looks down at the button around her neck.*) Peter! (*Takes a deep breath, defiant.*) I'll just have to do it on my own.

WENDY *starts wriggling out of her ropes, desperately trying to be free, it's heroic.* MRS DARLING *picks up her bag with renewed determination and sets off with purpose.* DOC SWAIN *enters, sees* WENDY *struggling and laughs.*

DOC SWAIN. Nice try, little lady. (*Grabs her and hoists her over his shoulder.*) Time for you to see the Captain.

DOC SWAIN *exits with* WENDY *over his shoulder.*

The LOST BOYS, MICHAEL *and* JOHN *all come charging in again. It's riotous fun, they are playing catch with a little toy pirate ship, snatching it and wrestling it from one another.*

PETER. Last one to the tree trunk is a loser!

The LOST BOYS *ignore* PETER, *still angry at his game.*

Hey? Hey? Want to hear what I did to Hook? Want to hear how he screamed?

The BOYS *all dash in around* PETER *and dash off.* MICHAEL *gets left behind, he's holding the toy boat. He stops.*

MICHAEL. Wait a second – I haven't seen Wendy for ages. Hey, John, where's /

TOOTLES (*shouting back*). / Come on, Michael; don't be a loser!

MICHAEL *charges off after the others.*

Scene Two

The Jolly Roger, *a terrifying barnacled and battered ship, sails on, and sits low in the dank lagoon. Mist hangs in the air, black unctuous water gulps at its hull. The ship is covered in* PIRATES *and the party is in full swing – accordions, pipes, lanterns swaying in the breeze. The* PIRATES *are dancing the hornpipe.* HOOK *lurks, discontented.*

SMEE. Come on, Captain, you beat him – we won. Treat yourself?

HOOK. I want to see my sword through him; I want to watch him take his last breath.

    SMEE *rubs* HOOK'*s shoulders.*

SMEE. He's gone. It's over.

HOOK. It's not – he's out there. I know it.

SMEE. It's time to – relax. We've been working for this, for years. We've earned this time, put our feet up – get a nice place in the sun –

HOOK. Never!

    A crow, shrill and clear and full of youthful energy sings out across the lagoon – followed by the sound of laughing children.

SMEE. No? M-might have been a crow?

    HOOK *slams his hook into the gunnel of the boat with ferocity – the* PIRATES *freeze.*

HOOK. Bring me the girl, Smee!

SMEE. No, Captain – there's no need, she's such a moaner /

HOOK. / Bring me the girl.

    The PIRATES *drag* WENDY *on deck. She's dressed in a glorious dress, spoils from some unlucky princess. She's bound and gagged but defiant, resisting them all the while.*

Shh, shh, shh – careful now, you'll ruin your pretty dress.

HOOK *removes* WENDY*'s gag.*

WENDY. Give me back my nightie.

HOOK. That old thing? But you look so… glamorous.

WENDY. I don't want your stupid dress or your gold or your grog – I want /

HOOK. / Yes?

WENDY *clams up and looks at her feet, she's biting back tears.* HOOK *lifts* WENDY*'s chin, gently, with his hook.*

Oh, sweetheart, I know how hard it is when you care about people and they disappoint you. You care about Peter very much and he didn't fight for you, did he?

WENDY. I don't want to talk about, P – P /

HOOK. / You had so much faith in him.

WENDY *nods tearfully.*

Your poor poor heart. But – you know – it was wasted on such a selfish and immature /

WENDY. / He does care – I – it's my fault really – I – I left the Home Under the Ground, I was just upset and I kept moaning and I – I shouldn't have left I – I should have just relaxed and had fun and /

HOOK. / I told him, after you left, I told him /

WENDY. / He's alive?

HOOK. Yes. He's alive – and I told him that we'd take you to the ship and that if he wanted you, he should come here to fight for you. But it seems…

WENDY. He knows where I am?

HOOK. What could be more important than coming to get you? Some silly game? Some adventure?

WENDY*'s head drops, defeated.*

Tell us where he is, Wendy. (*Beat*.) If you tell us where
he lives – we can hurt him just like he hurt you, hm? It's
only fair.

WENDY. I – I can't, I won't – I – won't.

HOOK. If you stayed here with us, Wendy – you know there's
no making breakfast or washing up, or mending socks – no
doing anything for anyone else… it's just *fun*.

WENDY. But who makes sure they don't get hungry? Who
cleans – who /

  HOOK *flips open a small chest of gold coins – runs them
  through his fingers.*

HOOK. / We pay for it. If you're cold, you buy some coal and
hire a boy to keep the damn thing stoked. If you're tired, you
buy yourself the biggest of beds and a boy to do the work
whilst you lay in!

  The PIRATES *guffaw, swig at their bottles, roll around the
  ship drunkenly, singing, swaying.*

WENDY. But how do you get the money?

HOOK. We… steal it.

WENDY. But that's wrong.

HOOK. Why?

WENDY. Because – you're taking from people without giving
them anything in return.

HOOK. All those boys, Wendy – don't they take and take? Take
breakfast, take stories, take medicine – and what do they
give you in return?

WENDY. They – they love me; they just… forget, sometimes.

HOOK. But do you *ever* forget them?

WENDY. Well… no.

HOOK. Well, perhaps, tonight you could have the night off?

  WENDY *shakes her head and steps back from him.*

  Bring out The Princess Chest, lads.

The PIRATES *bring in a large Chinoiserie wardrobe, an intricately decorated, beautiful, elegant chest – blacks and reds and golds, it is exotic and mystifying.* WENDY *tries to resist her curiosity – but it's too much.* HOOK *opens the doors of the chest to reveal a mirror.* WENDY *sees herself for the first time, she's overwhelmed – she's never seen herself looking so glamorous. General 'ooh'-ings and 'aaah'-ings from the* PIRATES. WENDY *twists and turns in her robes.*

Oh, Wendy.

WENDY. Wow… I look…

HOOK *reaches into the chest and takes out an elaborate crown, a bejewelled necklace – and places them on* WENDY.

HOOK. Don't you feel lovely and powerful and strong?

WENDY. Yes. Yes, yes I do!

HOOK. Don't you look a thousand times better than he made you feel?

WENDY. I –

HOOK. Strike up the band, boys! Let's dance the hornpipe; Wendy is aboard and in need of a party – LET'S GET DECADENT!

The ship bursts into full swing – it's uproarious, WENDY *is flung from pirate to pirate, she's wild with glee, it's delicious.* WENDY *stops a moment, suddenly melancholy. She looks at the button around her neck.*

Wendy, darling, what's the matter?

WENDY. Why, if you have everything you want to be happy, do you spend all your time chasing Peter?

HOOK. Your cup is empty, my dear – Dogs! Bring Wendy some more grog!

WENDY. No – I – I might just go and um – I feel a little…

WENDY *dashes off to the aft of the boat. She sits alone, confused.* HOOK *is irate, glares at her.* SMEE *guides him to the bow, muttering a plan.*

SMEE. Captain, this ain't going to work, she won't give 'im up.

HOOK. I made Mother Teresa dance on tables, Smee. Wendy is a thirteen-year-old girl.

SMEE. But it's – it's her 'eart. I think she... cares for him, Captain.

HOOK. Can you imagine it? Caring for someone else so much that you'd be willing to die for them? It's /

SMEE. / Amazing.

HOOK. Pathetic. Why doesn't anyone feel like that about me?

SMEE. They do.

HOOK. Like who?

SMEE. Me.

HOOK. Yes, I'm asking you.

SMEE. Me, sir.

HOOK. Yes, Smee – I'm asking you.

SMEE. Um...

HOOK. Oh, forget it. (*Sulks over to the bow and looks out to sea.*) How does he command such loyalty?

SMEE. Might just be how she feels.

HOOK. Feels?

SMEE. I reckon I've felt something similar.

 HOOK *turns to look at* SMEE *a little seriously.*

HOOK. You've felt like that?

SMEE. Yes.

HOOK. For whom?

SMEE. Oh, I don't know... you?

 Beat. The moment is held – it seems like HOOK *may finally have heard.*

HOOK. Stop asking me what *I* think, I'm asking *you* – you blathering idiot! Enough! Enough! I'll scheme us out of this on my own. Go and get me a bloody daiquiri.

SMEE *exits,* HOOK *howls at the sky.*

I will find you, Pan!

WENDY *sits at the other end of the ship.* MARTIN *approaches.*

MARTIN. You all right? You should probably get back to the party, Hook don't like a loner, makes him nervous.

WENDY. Oh yes, of course – I'm just doing my – hair – I /

MARTIN. / It's okay – listen – (*Pathetic, mouthwash gurgling sounding.*) Argghhhhh.

WENDY Is that your argghh?

MARTIN (*checks no one is listening*). Grog makes me sick, bruise like a peach, faint at the sight of blood. I don't fit, neither.

WENDY *gives* MARTIN *a big hug.* MARTIN *is a little confused.*

WENDY. Mother always says 'follow your heart' and 'trust your instinct' – but, you see – Hook has been so kind and generous and – but all this still feels – wrong somehow – and then Peter – Peter has done nothing right and yet somehow, I still – think he's –

MARTIN. Well – there you go.

WENDY. But it's not as easy as that because – my feelings won't stay still. I believe in Peter for a second and I feel all warm and I think of his eyebrows and his grin and when he's all like 'Wendy! Stretchy slug!' and I… and then it all changes and I'm angry because he didn't save me and I bet he's out there just laughing and playing not even thinking about me and then I remember when he made me laugh or said he'd play Father and – (*Looks at her button.*) and I believe in him again but I can't keep any one thought or feeling still for long enough to decide! All the characters in the stories that Mother reads have this moment where they

listen to their heart and they just know what's true and they
know what to do and – I – I keep having these very serious
talks with myself – 'Come on, Wendy – just decide' but I –
can't. I think I'm made wrong.

MARTIN. Okay, okay – wait – slow down or you're going
break your head. Look, stories are written by people that
already know the ending, they go back and fiddle with the
middle to make it match afterwards; they're cheating. When
you're right in the middle of it – no one knows their
aa-aardvark from their elbow –

WENDY. So what do I do?

MARTIN. You just do – something, anything – like if you jump
into the lagoon – and you get eaten by sharks, you'll know it
was the wrong thing to do.

WENDY. I don't want to get eaten by sharks.

MARTIN. You won't care if you get eaten, cos you'll be eaten
already. But if it's right – then you'll definitely know it was
right – cos you tested it.

WENDY. You're a very wise pirate.

MARTIN. But that's just it, Wenners, I don't reckon pirates are
meant to be wise.

WENDY. Maybe everyone is made wrong.

MARTIN. Or maybe we all just ain't in the right place yet –
we're in the middle – and when we get to the end we'll be
like: 'Oooohhhh yeah – now I see.' You know what – I once
overheard Smee and Hook talking about how Lost Boys
come to Neverland, how they land here.

WENDY. Lost Boys? They land? How? Tell me!

MARTIN. They just drop down from the sky and I suddenly I
thought maybe I'm meant to be a Lost Boy and not a pirate;
maybe I just landed in the wrong place.

WENDY. How do they land? What makes them /

MARTIN. / When Lost Boys get lost, they become stars – no
wait, shh /

WENDY. / Stars?

MARTIN. And they don't land on Neverland until their
    families /

WENDY. / Until their families what? Until their families what,
    Martin!

HOOK. Time to play, Wendy.

WENDY. Oh, I'm still quite tired, I –

HOOK. Now!

WENDY. Martin? Martin!

HOOK. Martin, go and clean the poop deck. We want to initiate
    you, to check you're a real pirate – so that we know you
    really do care about us the way we care about you.

WENDY. An initiation?

HOOK. Where can we find Peter?

WENDY. I – I don't know where he lives.

    WENDY *does the sound of snotfrogs.*

SMEE. What the burglemaloo was that?

HOOK. Sweetheart, that's a lie, isn't it?

WENDY. No. (*Snotfrogs.*)

HOOK. Let's see how kind that heart really is – dogs, shall we?
    Bring out the Picin Princess.

    HOOK *turns and reveals* TIGER LILY, *she's bound and
    gagged – and held by the* PIRATES.

WENDY. Tiger Lily.

    WENDY *dashes forward for* TIGER LILY *but* HOOK *holds
    her back.*

HOOK. No, no – don't forget, Wendy. She left you to die,
    remember? She didn't save you. You must stop wasting your
    affection on those that don't deserve it. It's terribly weak of
    you. Lower the plank.

WENDY. What? What are you doing?

TIGER LILY. Wendy – don't risk no skin for me, man. I'm not your fight.

HOOK. Now – tell us where Peter Pan lives or we'll kill Tiger Lily; hold her over the water, chaps.

The PIRATES *suspend* TIGER LILY.

Come on – quick quick, or else the croc will come and make the decision for you.

WENDY. He lives – um – he lives – can I think about it for a moment /

HOOK. / I've been so good to you.

WENDY. He lives /

HOOK. / Kill her.

The PIRATES *push* TIGER LILY *over, but just in time…*

WENDY. No! He lives in the Home Under the Ground – beneath the five trees in the clearing in the Never Forest.

SMEE. I don't bloody believe it.

HOOK. Hold it! Oh, darling Wendy – well done – well done!

HOOK *opens his arms to* WENDY. WENDY *stays stuck still.*

TIGER LILY. You saved me, over him?

WENDY. Jump.

MARTIN (*quietly*). Jump.

WENDY. Just jump. Jump! Now! Jump! We have to get there before he does!

WENDY *suddenly charges at* TIGER LILY, *who barely understands.* WENDY *grabs her hand and launches the pair of them over the side of the boat.*

WENDY/TIGER LILY. Aahhhhhhhhh!!!!!

HOOK. No! No!

MARTIN. Go, Wendy! Go! You jumped, you little hero!

All the PIRATES *turn on* MARTIN, *swords drawn.*

Oh. Bum. Wendy, wait for me!

MARTIN *runs and leaps off the plank after* TIGER LILY *and* WENDY.

HOOK. Don't just stand there – heave-ho, you useless swine! Get me to shore! Get me to the clearing!

MURT *unfortunately hesitates a moment and* HOOK *swipes him clean across the face in his rage, knocking him to the floor.*

Stop dawdling! I will find him and I will kill him!

HOOK *exits into the tender.*

Scene Three

The Home Under the Ground. PETER *bursts into the room, having been concealed in a bunk bed. He's screaming, wild and savage. The* BOYS *all scream and charge around after him. It's feral, wild.* PETER *turns on the* BOYS… *they're enraptured.*

PETER. His eyes are so wide with being afraid – these little bits of white at the corner of his mouth cos he's so tired, trying so hard, breathing so fast, panting and panting – but I keep stabbing – stabbing –

PETER *jabs at the* BOYS – *they gasp and push back.*

Stab! Stab! And he couldn't even get his hook out in time, he is just swiping and swiping and trying but – I've got him on the back foot and pow! Pow! Pow!

PETER *holds the sword up to* NIBS*'s neck, his eyes are wild, he's panting.*

– and I'm going to slice him in two – right there – that close, his skin all yellow – teeth all brown –

PETER *takes a breath a moment. Silence in the camp. The* BOYS *slightly afraid.*

MICHAEL. Peter? Where's Wendy?

PETER. I – was flying – I was so fast – so fast – I was like a bird – like a wolf and I'm telling you he was so – scared – so slow – and – and /

JOHN. / Did you – did you – kill him?

Pause. The BOYS *look at* PETER *their eyes wide with expectation, their faces hungry for drama.*

PETER. Ha! Ha ha! Ha ha ha!

PETER *takes out his harmonica and starts playing a killer tune. His feet are thumping. He's leaping, spinning, he crows. The* BOYS *all crow back, they all kick off, it's wild – foot-stamping, thigh-slapping. The* LOST BOYS *are stamping, jumping.* PETER *charges up onto a stage, something high. He's wild with it, spinning round and round. He entrances the* BOYS, *as if he's a rock star. The* BOYS *grab objects, they find a beat, they whoop, they wail, there's something brilliant, savage.* PETER *starts doing a Cossack dance, keeping his knees up – up. The* BOYS *chant and cheer – 'Peter! Peter! Peter!'* PETER *goes and goes – he's exhausted but he can't stop, he won't let himself stop. He spins and spins – he stumbles. The* BOYS *try to keep cheering but the younger ones are a little afraid –* PETER *goes and goes – he stumbles, he's panting. He tries – he's got nothing left. He tries – he grabs his side, he dances a little – he stands – he pants. The* BOYS *stop cheering.*

Go! Go!

NIBS. Peter?

PETER. Lead the training! It's Hook or me this time! We're going to fight – *go!*

The LOST BOYS, *in a frenzy, dash about wildly and grab their weapons. They're full of it – wired.* NIBS *marches them out of the Home Under the Ground.* PETER *stoops, his hands on his knees, he's exhausted, he grabs his side. He sits, breathless, collapses.* PETER *notices the bottle of medicine on the floor.*

Medicine, given by Mother once a day to show she cared.

PETER *looks at the bottle and feels terrible. He slams it down at his side.* PETER *spots* TINK's *light on in her cage – he starts thumping it with a stick.*

Tink! Tink! Get up!

TINK. I'm sleeping.

PETER. Come and play – we can play anything you like – anything at all?

TINK. Where are the boys?

PETER. Battles – upstairs. Play a game – come on – let's play!

TINK *clambers down and* PETER *trips her up – they go rolling across the floor. They end up hands and knees, face to face, their faces rather close. There is a moment –* TINK *is prepared for the one thing she's always wanted.* PETER *bursts out laughing and leaps up.*

I'm so glad you're simple and fun, Tink.

TINK. Yeah.

PETER. Do you know any good stories?

TINK. Not at the minute – I'm a bit out of stories.

PETER. Oh.

TINK. We could go tickle the stars or fly in the forest or pick on pixies. Just you and me? You remember that one time when we went to that fairy party up on the mountain and we smoked a little /

PETER. / Yeah yeah, mental.

TINK. Mackerel.

PETER. Oh yeah – actually, course.

TINK. And we had a pint /

PETER. / Yeah, man; wasted.

TINK. Of Neverberry juice.

PETER. Real waste, spilt loads of mine.

TINK. And we spent all evening making out /

PETER. / What?

TINK. Making out that we were savages – all the pixies got
really scared.

PETER. Oh yeah – yeah.

TINK. Just you and me, the old days. We have a right laugh,
don't we?

Beat.

PETER. Do you want to make a plan?

TINK. A plan? We never make plans. Plans are boring snoring,
Pete.

PETER. Yes, they are. You're right. You're right.

TINK. How about a crazy dance – you know – like –

*TINK goes mental – funky-chicken sort of rock-out mash-up.
PETER looks a moment, starts to laugh. They play together,
it's funny – it's fun. Then PETER does the same monkey
impression he did at WENDY the night she arrived.*

That's not dancing, that's monkey! Silly!

PETER. Oh, is it?

PETER stops dancing.

TINK. Don't matter though! We can both be monkeys!

*TINK pretends to be a monkey, but PETER looks at her like
it's not quite right.*

How about I – um – I tidy up – or – gosh – there, looks like
that trouser-knee needs patching, pass it 'ere, I'll have it
done in a jiffy.

Beat. PETER holds a thimble out to TINK. TINK takes it.

It's a thimble. I don't get it.

PETER. No. (*Beat.*) I stole some of your fairy dust.

TINK. I know.

PETER. I can't seem to have a happy thought. I think I've forgotten how to forget. I did a bad thing or – I did a – I – had to – I tried to /

TINK. / She's not dead, Pete.

PETER. What?

> *Beat.*

TINK. I've seen her.

PETER. Are you – are you telling the truth?

TINK. Yes.

PETER. Tink! Tink!

> PETER *leaps for joy – runs around, can't control himself, it's real relief, real delight. He grabs* TINK *and all the while,* TINK *stands quite still and watches.*

Where is she?

TINK. She's at the lagoon.

PETER. Is she okay? She's all right?

TINK. Yeah.

PETER. They haven't hurt her?

TINK. No.

PETER (*heading for the door*). I'll just apologise, I'll explain – I'll just say, I'm sorry for leaving you to die at the hands of pirates and she'll be happy and we'll get the Lost Boys and come back here and play Mother and Father and I'll make a plan, no – no – I'll let her make a plan and everything will be all right.

> PETER *makes a dash for the door.*

TINK. She was in some swanky dress dancing the 'ornpipe with a boatload of pirates.

> PETER *stops suddenly.*

PETER. What?

TINK. Saw her doin' the hokey-cokey with 'ook 'imself; she was laughing.

PETER. Laughing?

TINK. She looked... happy.

PETER *charges for the door,* TINK *steps in his way.*

No, don't, Pete – you'll make a monkey of yourself – you turn up there and she don't want saving and Hook's going to laugh right in your face.

PETER. She was dancing... with Hook?

TINK. No – you'll look like a 'naana.

PETER. Move, Tink.

TINK. I'm saving you from yourself.

PETER. Get out my way –

TINK. Pete, no!

TINK *throws a lot of fairy dust in* PETER*'s face. He stumbles, he swoons, he falls down.*

Oh oh – I think I used a bit much – Pete? Come on – wakey-wakey – it's just a bit of fairy dust – I'm sorry – I – oh, bum, he's out cold. Pete?

There's a noise in one of the entrance trees. TINK *dashes over.*

Oh no, it's the boys – now Nibs, it's going look bad but – (*Freezes.*) That don't sound like Nibs... (*Dashes back over to* PETER.) Peter – you got to wake up, you hear me? You got to wake up now, Peter! Oh no – I'm so sorry –

TINK *looks around her desperately – there's someone at the door.*

Go small, Tink – go small – I can't I'm too full of 'fraid. Oh, bum.

TINK *hides.* HOOK *enters, cautiously – his sword raised. He sees* PETER.

HOOK. Look, he's sleeping. His precious medicine from Mummy right by his side.

HOOK *holds up the medicine and a bottle with skull and crossbones from which he takes three vile yellow drops*.

Night night – Peter Pa–

PETER *moans in his sleep*. HOOK *freezes, stares at the boy*.

What lurks in that empty-seeming head? (*Bends close*.) I don't want your life, your charm – I don't even want your youth. I want your time, Peter. Give me your time. Time again – time to make mistakes, time to be unsure – a time when errors were lessons not failures. When things could still turn out all right; oh, Peter – you lucky thing – take me back to endlessness… take me back to a time before I was aware of time.

HOOK *drops the poison into the medicine, leaves the medicine by* PETER*'s side and exits*. PETER *sits bolt upright in bed, a little woozy. He reaches for the medicine and goes to glug it*. TINK *bursts out of the cupboard and knocks the medicine from his hand, they both go tumbling*.

PETER. Stop it! I'm going to find Wendy! Give me the medicine!

PETER *grabs it back and goes to drink it*. TINK *grabs it*.

TINK. No, Peter –

PETER. Give it!

PETER *grabs it back off* TINK and *puts it to his lips*.

TINK. No!

TINK *grabs the medicine again and glugs it down*.

PETER. Tink? Tink, your – your light is going out. Tink? Tink! Please don't die, Tink… please. (*Pause – thinks*.) I need children to believe in fairies, it's the only thing that will bring her back. (*Drops to his knees and appeals to the audience*.) To all the boys and girls that are dreaming of Neverland – listen, please – I need your help. If you can hear me – I need you to believe in fairies. Do you hear? I need

you to squeeze your eyes shut and see them in your heads
and know – I need you to believe, if you believe she'll come
back to life. If you believe in fairies, clap your hands –
please, we must save Tink – clap your hands!

PETER *keeps his eyes shut and claps his hands furiously –
he uses all his might and energy. The audience begins to
clap – as hard and as fast as they can. Tiny LEDs have been
placed around the audience so, as the children clap, it seems
that fairies are hidden in every seat, that they are nestled
between all the children. For a moment the stage suddenly
seems full of fairies – before – whoosh – they are gone. The
lights are out, the fairies are alive and well and off to new
adventures.* TINK *springs back up to life.*

TINK. What's going on here then?

PETER. Uh – wow – thank – okay. Phew. I thought you were
dead.

TINK. Oh, that – ner – barely a hiccough.

PETER. I don't think I should play with any more girls. They
all seem to die.

TINK. Peter? Thank you.

PETER. What for?

TINK. The resuscitation.

PETER. You saved my life.

TINK. And you saved mine.

PETER. Of course I did. You're Tink, you're my fairy.

TINK. Oh, Peter, that's –

PETER *grabs* TINK *and gives her a huge hug.*

Pete?

PETER. Yeah.

TINK. Go and save Wendy. Go and save her. I'll tell the boys –
we'll follow. Go.

PETER *hugs* TINK *once more and leaps out of the Home
Under the Ground – he's on a mission.*

TINK *stands a moment. She sniffles, wipes a tear from her eye.*

(*To audience*.) Shut up – I got summink in my eye, that's all – it's nuffink. (*Sniffs again and turns honestly to the audience. Tries to smile, shrugs*.) Just the way the cookie crumbles, eh?

There is a sound at the entrance to the Home Under the Ground.

Scene Four

TINK *dashes to the door.*

TINK. Pete! You came back, you –

WENDY *enters, she's soaked, bedraggled, exhausted.*

Oh, it's you.

WENDY. Where's Peter?

TINK. Right – turn around – back to the *Jolly Roger* – Out! Out!

WENDY. Where's Peter, Tink? Has Hook been here? Did he – is Peter okay?

TINK. Yes, Hook has been here –

WENDY. No?

TINK. And yes Peter's alive – no thanks to you.

WENDY (*relief for a second, then…*). Well, don't try and protect him because I'm telling you when I find him – I am going to – I am going to – he better be ready because I – I am – angry – and I am going to /

TINK. / You're genuinely terrifying.

WENDY. He drags me here, promising to help me, gives me a blinkin' button – plays monkeys – then he lies to me, leaves me for dead – he didn't try and rescue me – he – he /

TINK. / And now he's en route to the *Jolly Roger* to save your skinny ass.

WENDY. What?

TINK. Right. So move.

WENDY. But I'm not there.

TINK. Your powers of perception are overwhelming. I got to go and tell the Lost Boys they're on back-up and quick or it's Peter going solo versus a boatload of pirates.

TINK *goes to barge past* WENDY. WENDY *steps in her way*.

WENDY. No.

TINK. Look, I know you got the 'ump with 'im but /

WENDY. / No! Wait. We –

TIGER LILY *enters*.

TINK. Oh great – good – invited the whole island, did we? PS, Wendy – how did Hook know where we live?

WENDY. He's been here –

TIGER LILY. I can smell him.

TINK. You what?

WENDY. I – made a little –

TINK. A little... a little blab? Did you? Did you go a bit funny? Lack of oxygen up there on your high horse?

TIGER LILY. Look, 'scuse me but –

WENDY. I had to – I had no choice – I /

TIGER LILY. / You kind of did.

TINK. And all along she's a blinkin' turncoat.

TIGER LILY. Will you two just shut up.

WENDY. Oh, I'm the one with questionable morals, am I?

TIGER LILY *imitates* WENDY*'s line in a whiney voice*.

TINK. And now we got to rebuild our *whole* house!

WENDY. You tried to kill me!

TINK (*gasp, outrage*). I did not!

WENDY. Tootles told me, you liar.

TINK. You are so judgemental.

WENDY. Excuse me!

TIGER LILY. You are pretty judgemental.

TINK. Well, this has – as usual – been a joy but I got to go and save some lives /

TIGER LILY. / I got you this far. I done my job, now I'm going to fight –

Something snaps – WENDY stands in the doorway and waves a stick around aggressively, and slightly crazily, at the two girls. They stand bemused.

WENDY. No. No. No. No. No. No! No one's going anywhere. I've had it with this island. Every single girl I've met has tried to kill me; do you know how that makes me feel? Tink, you've never liked me and I've not done anything to you ever. And, Tiger Lily, just get over the Lone Ranger thing – you might be able to do it on your own but isn't it just… better, to have some help? I don't get it – I don't get why the boys get to be friends and have fun and – but we – we have to be against each other. And if it's all because of – him – well – well, that – that's a waste… because I promise you – he isn't not being friends or not having fun because of us, is he? And the truth is – I would love to fight like you, or be all – (*Makes a gesture and a noise that indicates 'grr' and great and bolshy and brilliant.*) like you, I – actually – think you're both – quite… I'd like to be like you. So here's what's going to happen – we're going to be a team. We're going to go to that pirate ship, we're going to kick some pirate – bum – and we're going to find my little brother and I – I – will be Captain. Who's with me?

Pause. TIGER LILY and TINK sulk a little. TINK shrugs.

TINK. 'Spose.

TIGER LILY. Um…

WENDY. I said, who's with me?

TIGER LILY. If you gunna fight you got to lose the dress.

WENDY goes to pull it straight off.

TINK. Whoa, missus! My eyes.

TIGER LILY. I mean change it up – not freaking – get ya nuddy out. Tch.

WENDY. I do apologise; I got a little overexcited.

TINK. I'll get the weapons chest.

TIGER LILY. Looks like we got us some fighting to do.

TIGER LILY puts her hand into the centre of the group – the other two cautiously lay theirs on top. The three of them roar – it's a battle cry, it's solidarity – it's brilliant.

TINK. I'll get the weapons chest. Wendy?

WENDY. Yeah?

TINK. I'm sorry.

WENDY. Come on.

The three of them ready themselves for battle. WENDY *and* TIGER LILY *leave.*

TINK. Wait for me!

MARTIN enters, TINK *draws her sword.*

Back off, you rancid little /

MARTIN. / No – no, I'm with Wendy – I followed her – I – I – she said get a sword – I – Nice wings.

TINK. Who are ya?

MARTIN. I'm M-martin. Who are you?

TINK. Who am I? Who am I? I'll tell you who I bleedin' /

MARTIN (*grins coyly*). / Come on, there ain't no one that don't know who Tink is, eh?

TINK (*coy, shoves him – a little over-hard*). Shut up.

MARTIN. Most famoustest fairy there is… bit star-struck.

They blush and look at their feet – sparks. MARTIN *sneezes all over* TINK.

Oh – oh – b – b – oh – so – oh –

MARTIN *tries to mop up* TINK *but sort of dabs her boobs and gets all of a muddle.*

TINK. S'all right, love a sneezer. (*Offers him a tissue.*) Come on, snotty – there's work to do.

TINK *and* MARTIN *exit.*

Scene Five

In the misty twilight of the clearing, the LOST BOYS *are sparring – covered in warpaint and dressed in forest-made uniforms. They are sweating, they are training hard.* SLIGHTLY *is stationed as lookout, telescope in hand.* NIBS *is the commanding officer, overseeing the training.*

NIBS. Slightly, the report?

SLIGHTLY. The *Jolly Roger* is still in the south of the lagoon, sir – but the sun is almost down.

NIBS. We need to move out.

MICHAEL. But Peter isn't here yet.

JOHN *and* NIBS *face off, looking askance at one another.*

JOHN. Someone's going to have to step up.

NIBS. That they are.

JOHN. Wonder who it's going to be?

NIBS. I wonder.

JOHN. Who indeed?

CURLY. Well… it's going to be one of you two, in't it.

JOHN *and* NIBS *aggressively put their fists out as if they're going to fist fight. A beat. Tension before the first punch – and then they play rock-paper-scissors. They draw – choosing the same thing. There's wild tension, they both reach for their swords, when…* MARTIN *comes tearing out of the undergrowth. The* BOYS *round on him.*

NIBS. Pirate!

BOYS. Kill him!

MARTIN. No – no – please – stop!

SLIGHTLY. Draw your sword, cabin boy!

MARTIN. Stop – I'm not a pirate – I'm not – (*Panting, can't catch his breath.*)

JOHN. Nice try, you barnacled blundering buccaneer!

   MARTIN *does an arrgggh – it's pathetic. The* BOYS *stop.*

CURLY. Oh.

MARTIN. Look, listen – I've been trying to find you for – I've got a message from Tink –

JOHN. Come on, deep breaths.

MARTIN. It's my asthma, it's – woo – okay – okay – Hook captured Wendy.

   The BOYS *gasp.*

But then Peter arrived.

   The BOYS *cheer.*

But then Peter didn't save her.

   The BOYS *gasp.*

But then Wendy saved herself and Tiger Lily.

   The BOYS *cheer.*

But then Wendy told Hook where the Home Under the Ground is.

   The BOYS *gasp.*

But then Hook didn't kill Peter.

The BOYS *cheer*.

But then Peter went to fight Hook.

The BOYS *gasp*.

And then Wendy went to fight Hook.

The BOYS *gasp*.

But now we can all go together and help them!

The BOYS *gasp*.

No, that's good news, you should cheer –

The BOYS *back away from* MARTIN. MARTIN *is confused*.

Boys, it's good news, it's –

From behind MARTIN *out of the undergrowth come the*
PIRATES.

They're behind me, aren't they?

MARTIN *turns around and joins the* LOST BOYS – *they*
draw their swords.

DOC SWAIN (*in hushes*). One – two – three.

DOC SWAIN, MURT *and* JONES *charge on the* LOST
BOYS. TOOTLES *is the first to rush forward – screaming*
and bellowing with conviction – JONES *has him in seconds*
and binds him tight.

JOHN. Michael – attack – attack, you have to!

MICHAEL (*drops to the floor puts his hands over his ears and*
scrunches his eyes shut). Hydrogen, helium, lithium
beryllium, boron.

DOC SWAIN *slowly but surely binds him.* JOHN *leaps*
straight for DOC SWAIN, *bellowing with primal rage*.

DOC SWAIN (*nonchalantly pushing* JOHN *to the floor*). So
angry for one so young.

NIBS *is face to face with* DOC SWAIN, *who draws out a*
scalpel and a hatchet.·

NIBS. I'm not afraid of you, you swine!

DOC SWAIN laughs and holds the hatchet high until NIBS quivers and quakes and is easily caught. SLIGHTLY collides with MURT and knocks him over. SLIGHTLY offers his hand to help him up.

SLIGHTLY. I'm terribly sorry, that was such bad form – you're at an unfair disadvantage and I shouldn't have –

In his fussing MURT turns the offer of help into SLIGHTLY's capture.

Bad form – I say – bad form!

JONES. Captain wants them back at the ship… alive.

DOC SWAIN. But I was about to make my first incision.

MURT (*pops the paper bag MARTIN is using to appease his asthma attack*). Up – traitor!

NIBS shrinks from the blade. Deathly silence – then the PIRATES burst into cackles.

JONES. Heave-ho – let's be takin' them back to Captain!

The PIRATES pack up the BOYS – bind them tight and sling them over their shoulders and march off, whistling and cackling as they go.

ACT FOUR

Scene One

The Jolly Roger *sails into the lagoon* – HOOK *and* SMEE *stand aboard, looking triumphantly out to sea.*

SMEE. Look at it, look at it, Captain – everything you can see – you own, no more Pan – you're unrivalled, king of this island – at last – it's our playground.

HOOK. Neverland is mine!

SMEE. Ours?

HOOK. Mine mine mine!

SMEE. And once the dogs round up them Lost Boys, it'll be ours to settle down in – perhaps, you see, now I've been thinking about it a little while and I thought perhaps we could build a little cottage, I've collected some swatches and –

SMEE *unravels endless paint/fabric colour swatches, elaborate plans.*

HOOK. It's strange, you know, Smee – I – I've wanted for so long to be the fastest, the strongest, the greatest –

SMEE. I was thinking a soft waffle for the carpets and elephant's breath for the walls and /

HOOK. / I always imagined that I would feel – invincible.

SMEE. Captain – Peter Pan is dead… you're a legend. 'Captain Hook – the most brilliant buccaneer there ever was' ever, Captain – do you hear me? And that boy, that boy won't be but a smudge in the history books.

HOOK. Not a smudge.

SMEE. Captain?

HOOK. Can you hear that, Smee? There? Can you hear? That strange melancholy sound as if the mermaids are… crying?

SMEE. Captain!

HOOK. A sort of soft, lonely, wailing –

SMEE. Captain – look! It ain't mermaids – it's the snivelling blinkin' Lost Boys! The dogs have done it! They got 'em! All the Lost Boys! Oh, Captain!

HOOK. Yes, yes – a little more blood – a little more battle before bedtime.

The PIRATES *bring on the* LOST BOYS – *laughing, cackling, delighted.*

JONES. Where do you want 'em, Captain?

HOOK. Lower the plank. Lower the lovely jubbly little plank!

DOC SWAIN. But. Captain – surely we deserve a little – (*Holding up a large surgical instrument.*) playtime?

MICHAEL. Mother!

MURT. Scream as loud as you like; no one gunna hear ya under water.

HOOK *surveys the line of* BOYS, *peering – glaring.*

JOHN. Good God, you're ugly up close.

HOOK. Davey Jones's locker has got your name on it.

NIBS. Surely it's got Davey Jones's name on it.

HOOK (*snapping round*). Impudent little – (*Runs his hook along* TOOTLES*'s face.*) such beautiful youth... kill them! Kill them all!

The PIRATES *close in on the* BOYS – *cackling. Suddenly a crowing.* HOOK *freezes.*

No! No!

He turns slowly to see PETER *rising up from the gunnels – sword brandished, tick-tocking as he goes.*

PETER. Sorry to interrupt the party.

HOOK. I dreamt that you were dead.

PETER. Should have killed me when you had the chance – cos now I'm awake and I want to play!

HOOK. No! No!

PETER *crows*.

PETER. Tell me where Wendy is and I'll make it slightly less painful than it was going to be.

HOOK *lunges at* PETER, *they clash*. PETER *gets the advantage*.

MICHAEL. Peter!

DOC SWAIN (*holding his sword to the throat of the* BOYS). Back off, Pan!

PETER *looks up and the* PIRATES *have their swords at the throats of all the* LOST BOYS.

HOOK. One more move and their blood is on your hands.

JOHN. In war some men must fall.

PETER *drops his sword*.

Come 'ere – you little imp.

TOOTLES. No.

HOOK. Bind him, Smee!

SMEE *scuttles in and ties* PETER *to the mast*. HOOK, *meanwhile, takes* PETER *by the throat*.

You are going to watch the fear in the faces of every one of your precious little boys and then – I'm going to feed you, piece by piece – to the –

JONES. Um – C-captain – there, um –

HOOK. Shut up, Jones, I'm having my moment.

From the sky is the tremendous trio – WENDY, *flanked by* TINK *and* TIGER LILY, *in full battle gear*.

TIGER LILY. Boooooooooooom tang!

TINK. 'Ello, boys!

WENDY. BOG OOOFFFFFFF!!

*WENDY swings in and lets out a death-defying ROAR –
it's unimaginable such a big sound has come from such a
little person.*

PETER. Wendy?

HOOK. No? No! No!

JOHN. Blimey, that's my – sister.

WENDY. Looks like you might be in need of a bit of a… plan?
John, catch!

*The GIRLS land, whoop and charge! It's full fury – they all
know exactly what to do.*

John, catch!

*WENDY throws a dagger to JOHN. DOC SWAIN tries to
grab it.*

DOC SWAIN. Oi! Gimme that!

*DOC SWAIN doesn't get to the knife in time. JOHN catches
it and slices through his ropes. The PIRATES try to stop
them but to no avail – the BOYS are free, fighting breaks
out. TIGER LILY drops in front of HOOK and starts
sparring impressively with him.*

TINK lands on the boat.

HOOK. Shoot that fairy!

*SMEE shoots at TINK – TINK disappears up into the sky
again.*

TIGER LILY. Party time – old man.

WENDY. Boys!

PETER. Tiger Lily! Help!

TIGER LILY. Oooh – oooh – say it again, Peter! Say it again!
It's like music!

PETER. He's taken my sword! Untie me!

TIGER LILY *ignores him and keeps sparring with* HOOK.
WENDY *makes it to a crowd of* LOST BOYS, *huddles
them in and delivers the plan – a little like an American
football coach.*

MICHAEL. Wendy, I am so glad of you.

WENDY *whispers into* MICHAEL*'s ear.*

WENDY. Got it? Clear? Tink will guide you. Tink?

TINK*'s light appears and* MICHAEL *jumps into the water.
With* TINK *guiding his way,* MICHAEL *swims away.*

Tootles?

TOOTLES. Got it!

WENDY. Swim, Michael! Swim! Curly with Tiger Lily – take
Martin for recon. Tiger, now!

TIGER LILY *spins – throws* WENDY *her sword.*

TIGER LILY. He's all yours.

TIGER LILY *nods affirmation at* WENDY *– it's all
understood.* TIGER LILY *dashes off with* CURLY *and*
MARTIN *on a separate project.* WENDY *catches the sword
– and is faced with* HOOK.

HOOK. Careful – it's rather heavy, don't cut yourself.

WENDY *roars and clashes with* HOOK.

WENDY. Raaaaaa!

HOOK *is pushed back.*

HOOK. My God, she's rather good –

PETER. Wendy! Wendy! I'm /

WENDY. / All tied up?

PETER. Wendy! Quick!

WENDY. Just relax, Peter, unwind!

PETER. Wendy – I'm serious! Wendy!

WENDY. Don't worry – you don't have to do anything – just be very very scared, then very very impressed, then very very grateful.

HOOK *gets the better of* WENDY. *The* BOYS *are overpowered for a moment, the* PIRATES *are on top.*

JOHN. Wendy, they're winning!

WENDY. Michael, now! Now!

The PIRATES *rush at the* BOYS *but* MICHAEL *swings in from the galleries – followed by a cloud of fireflies, who he directs as he goes. The* PIRATES *are dazzled.*

JOHN. He's flying.

MICHAEL. I found my happy thought! I'm flying.

JONES. It's every bloody firefly on the island!

MICHAEL. Photinus – go left! Luciola – right!

MURT. I can't see a thing, even in me good eye!

DOC SWAIN. I'm blind! I'm blind!

MICHAEL. Phausis Reticulata – hold your position!

HOOK *scrambles to the armaments chest and throws pistols to all the* PIRATES. TIGER LILY, MARTIN *and* CURLY *have just finished their work and they scamper away.* MICHAEL *lands back on deck.*

HOOK. Dogs! Get your guns! Shoot them out of the sky, God damn it – shoot them!

All the PIRATES *grab their guns and point them at the fireflies.*

JONES. My gun ain't workin'.

MURT. Nor mine.

HOOK. Shoot them!

HOOK *struggles with his own gun – hand and hook proving tricky.* JONES *and* MURT *look down their own barrels, and shoot. The guns explode, covering them with custard.*

JONES. Custard?

CURLY. Cuuuuuuusssssssttttaaaaarrrrddddd!!

HOOK. You bloody idiots! Swain – no!

> DOC SWAIN, *two seconds later, fires his, covering him with custard. The entire pirate crew, bar* HOOK, *is doused in yellow.*

> For God's sake.

> *Bang!* HOOK *shoots the fireflies.*

> The cannons, fire the cannons!

> *The* PIRATES *dash up to the back deck and start wheeling out the cannons.* HOOK *shoots his gun at last and the fairy clouds disperse.* TOOTLES *is standing at the bottom of the mast, looking up, his knees knocking.*

WENDY. Go, Tootles. I know you can do it.

TOOTLES. Come on, Tootles – come on. (*Scrunches up his eyes and grits his teeth and starts climbing up the mast.*) Just don't look down.

TIGER LILY. Operation custard complete.

HOOK. Fire! Fire!

> TIGER LILY *and* WENDY *high-five. The cannon ball fires, at first it hits everything in sight, breaking things, bouncing off things, people diving everywhere, then – in a flash –* TINK *appears, larger than life.*

TINK. I got it!

> TINK *slam-dunks it into the water giving the* PIRATES *that had just about recovered from the custard a second dousing.*

HOOK. Shoot that fairy!

> HOOK *shoots at* TINK *and she disappears back into the air.*

WENDY. Tootles, now!

> TOOTLES, *up in the crow's nest, releases the sail and it comes billowing down over the* PIRATES. *The* LOST BOYS *wrestle the sail around the* PIRATES. *Using it like a clothes line, they manage to push all of the* PIRATES, *one by one,*

over the edge of the boat. It looks as if the BOYS *have won when…* HOOK *breaks free and aims his gun at* WENDY. TIGER LILY *sees it.*

TIGER LILY. Wendy? No!

HOOK *shoots* WENDY. TIGER LILY *leaps in the way and takes the bullet.*

WENDY. Tiger Lily! No!

TIGER LILY. Thank you – Wendy. You have been a good friend. I am off to see my family.

TIGER LILY *dies. Those on board stop and stare.* WENDY, *in a fit of passion, tries to grab* HOOK*'s gun from him but fails.*

WENDY. No!

HOOK. Now, now, Wendy, you're being irrational.

SMEE *appears from the cabin, holding another two guns.* HOOK *holds his gun at* WENDY *and the* BOYS. *Suddenly, the pair owns the deck and has everyone held at gunpoint.*

Now, why don't we all just calm down? (*Closes on the* BOYS.) Into the hold, all of you.

HOOK *pushes them into the hold, bolting the door shut.* TOOTLES, *meanwhile, has cut* PETER*'s ropes and freed him.* TOOTLES *remains cowering in the crow's nest.* PETER *leaps down on deck in front of* HOOK. HOOK *holds his gun at* PETER.

PETER. Oh, hello.

HOOK. So glad you could join us.

HOOK *drops his gun and pulls his sword.* SMEE *has* WENDY *held perilously over the side of the boat.*

SMEE. Stand down – now – or she goes in the drink.

WENDY. Peter, the crocodile – is right there!

PETER *stands, torn between the two.*

HOOK. Oh dear – Hook or Wendy – what a decision? Do you know I have the strangest feeling of déjà vu?

WENDY. Peter?

PETER *can't decide – he's in agony.* HOOK *slices at a guy-rope and a sail unfurls.*

HOOK. Imagine, Peter.

HOOK *uses his sword to cut a scene in the sail. We see* WENDY, *a woman now and happy, singing to a baby in her arms.*

Imagine your future.

PETER *stands, dazzled. A* MAN *arrives into the scene, dressed in a suit – tired from a day at work, he kisses her on the cheek and looks at the child.*

Imagine what she'd make of you; so tired, so serious. King of no one, prince of nothing – no more fun, no more games. Every day the same suit, the same office; always having to do things that you don't want to do. You'll never be a hero – ever again.

PETER. Who's that – man?

WENDY. Peter?

HOOK. All that – responsibility.

PETER *can't stand it, he feels like his head is going to explode.*

PETER. I don't want to be /

HOOK. / Of course you don't.

A SHADOW *appears at the window in the scene.*

PETER. Who's that – at the window? No – don't close the window – no!

OLDER WENDY, *in the image, goes and closes the window and leaves the room with her husband. The* SHADOW *remains.*

SMEE. Surrender!

WENDY. Save me, Peter!

HOOK. Choose her and no one will remember you.

PETER *leaps for* WENDY.

PETER. Wendy!

SMEE *pushes* WENDY *overboard.* PETER *dashes forward and grabs* WENDY *in the nick of time, it's heroic, he hauls her back on deck and lifts her up to safety.* PETER *turns,* WENDY *in one arm, and fights* SMEE *off.*

WENDY. Thank you.

PETER. Let's play, old man!

HOOK. Raaaaa!

PETER *turns on* HOOK *and* SMEE*, lunging at* HOOK*.* SMEE *sacrifices himself and leaps in the way of* PETER*'s blade.* SMEE *starts to fly up – up – into the sky.*

PETER. He's flying?

WENDY. It's his happy thought – sacrificing himself for Hook is his happy thought.

SMEE. See you in Timbuktu, Captain – I'll put up the tent.

HOOK. Oh, Smee – I never knew.

HOOK *draws his sword.* PETER *turns on* HOOK *and the old rivals go head to head.* HOOK *jabs at* PETER *and nearly gets him,* PETER *stumbles backwards.* HOOK *cackles.* PETER *goes for* HOOK *and knocks his sword out of his hand.*

HOOK *goes forward to pick up his sword but stays bent a little too long.*

PETER. You're tired?

PETER *can hardly stand it.* PETER *picks up* HOOK*'s sword and throws it to him.* HOOK *goes for* PETER *and misses.* PETER *drives* HOOK *right to the end of the plank. The* CROCODILE *appears, large and unctuous – with its 'tick-tock, tick-tock', getting ever louder.* PETER *and* HOOK *teeter nervously on the plank.*

Pirate killer, prince of the seas, demon of the skies!

PETER *crows loudly – he is youth, he is brilliance. He swipes at* HOOK *one last time – the blade goes right through his middle. The* LOST BOYS *cheer.* HOOK *grabs* PETER*'s hand before he retracts his sword and holds him – eye to eye – as he teeters on the end of the plank.*

HOOK. And you, Peter Pan... are becoming – a man.

PETER. Never!

PETER *pushes* HOOK *in anger, refusal – there's animal defiance in it.* HOOK *falls backward off the plank and into the jaws of the hungry* CROCODILE. PETER *stands and watches him go.* WENDY *looks a little sadly at* PETER. TINK *lands back on deck and lets the* BOYS *out from the hold. The* BOYS *cheer wildly. A party breaks out.* PETER *stands alone and looks a little sad.*

MICHAEL. Do you know, I never thought I had it in me to be a pirate-killer. I thought you would just do all the running and fighting and I would just watch. It's funny, isn't it? Imagining you might be quite different to what you always thought.

JOHN. Hm.

MICHAEL. Are you all right?

JOHN. Well... strangest thing, just whilst we were fighting there – I – I ended up allying with that Tiger Lily for a little moment and – I had this sort of – vision – of her ironing my handkerchiefs and listening to me tell her some very interesting things. And I can't tell you how pleasant it was. And then – she's – gone. Terribly confusing; think I need a jolly good ball game to sort me out.

WENDY *approaches* PETER.

PETER. Hello, Mother, how are you? Have you had a very hard day? They boys all seem well even after such an eventful time, they will sleep well tonight, won't they. Shall we return home and sit by the fire and talk of our days?

WENDY *looks at* PETER *a little quizzically a moment.*

WENDY. What do you want to do, Peter?

PETER. Why, I should sit by the fire and talk of my day as all good fathers do.

WENDY. No, Peter; what do you *want* to do?

Pause. PETER looks at his feet a moment, he is confused.

PETER. I don't know.

WENDY. Well... I want to know where my brother is and you – you know and –

PETER *plays monkey a little bit* – WENDY *softens.*

I'm serious – I –

PETER. This way.

WENDY. Where are we going?

PETER. Close your eyes, biscuit face.

PETER *takes* WENDY*'s hand for the first time.* WENDY *opens her eyes. They both step onto a cloud – the cloud lifts up, up into the sky.* PETER *wickedly stands up – the cloud starts to rock,* WENDY*, terrified, grabs onto the cloud.*

WENDY. No, Peter – look, it's not funny – I haven't got any fairy dust – I can't fly without it – stop it – look, it's getting late and we've had a very long day and – (*Suddenly stops panicking and looks up and the sky around her, she's captivated.*) Oh, look – it's – amazing.

PETER. See.

They look at each other a moment. PETER *points to the button around* WENDY*'s neck.*

Look – my kiss.

WENDY. I've kept it, all the time, ever since you gave it to me.

PETER. Oh.

WENDY. Have you kept mine?

PETER. Oh... um, no I – I – (*Checks his pockets.*) No I don't think I have. I must have –

WENDY. Forgotten it.

PETER. Yes – somewhere. I suppose.

WENDY. You just forget everything – just like that and it isn't fair because I remember everything – every last detail – all the time and /

PETER. / Well don't.

WENDY. What?

PETER. Remembering is mean.

WENDY. No it's not. It's forgetting all the time that's horrid.

PETER. Remembering is old and heavy and it feels all ugh inside.

WENDY. But forgetting is cold and heartless and awful and /

PETER. / I was lost once.

WENDY. You had a family?

PETER. Yes. I went back to see my mother – I flew right up to her window so I might look at her for a little while, just to see, just, well – I missed her. And there she was – and my old bedroom, my cot – and it was so lovely to see her face but –

WENDY (*gently*). But?

PETER. There was a new boy, a new baby in my cot where I had been and there was Mother and Father laughing and playing and dancing with big smiles on their faces.

WENDY. Peter, that's awful.

PETER. No, Wendy – don't you see? It's wonderful. It's the best thing ever.

WENDY. But that must have hurt so much.

PETER. Look at the stars. What are they made of?

WENDY. Um, Michael knows, it's dust and fire or something.

PETER. No – *look*. Really look.

WENDY *squints and looks at them.*

WENDY. That's strange – it's like they're shimmering – like they're made of – water? Pools of water?

PETER. When a boy gets lost, I take him up into the night sky and he becomes the newest smallest star. Look – like that one, just there.

WENDY. It's tiny.

PETER. The reason the stars shine is because each star is a Lost Boy reflecting his mother's tears as she looks up into the night, wishing him back. That's why they look like they are made of water.

WENDY. But that's so sad and the stars are so beautiful.

PETER. It's not really sad – the Lost Boys get to watch over their old families for a while and see that they are okay.

WENDY. But they're stuck, they can't get down. How, Peter? Please tell me how they are released. I so want to see Tom again, and Mother and Father will be so /

PETER. / At the very first moment that every member of the family has been truly happy again, for just one moment – that's all it takes, one second of pure happy, and the Lost Boy is released – he lands on Neverland and he is free to play – for ever.

WENDY. But I don't want to forget him. I love him.

PETER. You don't forget the boy; you just forget to be sad; just for a moment.

Pause.

WENDY. But I've been trying – I've been trying so hard to forget but I'm – I'm tired, Peter. I feel like I've been sad for such a long time... and I can't seem to /

PETER. / That's just it – you're trying and if you try to forget, well... That's why I couldn't tell you that forgetting was what you had to do – because if you knew, well, then you'd try – you'd try to forget – and, you see, if a person tries to forget it only makes them remember twice as hard and they get stuck /

WENDY. / No – Peter! You shouldn't have told me! Now I'll just try and try and never forget and Tom will stay stuck and /

PETER. / Just one happy thought – pure happy.

> WENDY *stops panicking. She looks at* PETER, *then she looks out at the night and from somewhere deep inside her she pulls the strongest bit of fight that she's ever found.* WENDY *stands – puts both feet on the edge of the cloud...*

WENDY. I am Wendy Darling. I am brave and I am strong and I am going on an adventure.

> WENDY *steps off the cloud and flies, soars out over the clouds – it's wonderful.*

Woohoo!!

> PETER *leaps off the cloud and flies with her – they swirl and swoosh.* PETER *crows.* WENDY *crows.*

Look – there – Peter! A shooting star!

> WENDY *turns to* PETER; *he is already looking at her as if he has seen something new.*

What?

PETER *kisses* WENDY.

A kiss?

Beat.

PETER. No. (*Blushes and looks away.*) That's a kiss – around your neck.

WENDY. Well, what was that, then?

> *Pause – they stare at one another – as if everything were understood and everything were possible if only* PETER *might kiss her again.*

> WENDY *moves toward* PETER *to touch him again but* PETER *pulls away.*

PETER. It is only make-believe – isn't it – that I am Father?

WENDY. Oh – um – of course.

PETER. I want to always be a little boy and to have fun.

> *Pause. They look at one another for a moment –* WENDY *is heartbroken.*

WENDY. Well, then... I shall leave you to play.

WENDY soars back down to the ship. PETER is left in the stars a little moment, he watches her go.

PETER. Wendy?

Scene Two

WENDY lands. The LOST BOYS, TINK, MICHAEL and JOHN have dressed up in pirates' gear and are having a great time pretending to be buccaneers – on the prow, at the wheel. MARTIN and TINK are in one corner together. The BOYS part and reveal TOM, beaming. WENDY sees him and can barely speak – tears fill her eyes, she doesn't want to touch him for fear he isn't real.

WENDY. Tom?

TOM. Hello, Wendy.

MICHAEL runs forward and hugs his little brother. JOHN holds his hand out. TOM goes to shake it – JOHN gives in and gives him a huge squeeze.

MICHAEL. Where have you been?

TOM. Oh – just – hanging around.

JOHN. I wish you'd been here for battle. I would have had you as my wingman.

MICHAEL. I could have shown you my fireflies – there were hundreds!

MICHAEL and JOHN step aside a little bit – WENDY has clear sight of her little brother.

WENDY. Come on, then.

WENDY holds her arms open and TOM runs into them. She squeezes him very tight – and has a little sniff of his hair. She gets a little teary.

It's very good to see you.

TOM. Thanks for getting me down.

WENDY. I'm so sorry I –

TOM *goes in for another ginormous hug and* WENDY *hugs him back.*

Mother and Father will be so – oh, come on – get your things – John, Michael – we're going home. We're taking Tom home.

The LOST BOYS *approach and crowd around* TOM, *slightly pushing* WENDY *backwards. The* LOST BOYS *inspect him as if he were some sort of specimen.*

TOOTLES. We can tell from his eyebrows.

SLIGHTLY. His feet are just the right size.

NIBS. He's got the height for bubble ball.

CURLY. And the look of a custard-lover.

MARTIN. Takes one to know one.

TOM. I do love custard – almost as much as cake. Talking of which, I'm very hungry.

WENDY. Of course, when we get home, Mother will cook us the most /

TOM. / I feel like I want – worms and custard.

SLIGHTLY. Good choice, old chap, good choice.

WENDY. But, Tom, we –

NIBS. He's a Lost Boy.

CURLY. You can just – tell.

WENDY. No, he's Tom Darling and –

TINK. We'll look after him – promise.

TOM. Isn't it fun?

WENDY. Yes.

TOM *gives* WENDY *another squeeze and then he's away.*

NIBS. Full formation for operation ambush!

TOM. But I don't know – how – I –

TOOTLES. Don't worry, I'll show you how.

NIBS puts his hat on TOM's *head. The* LOST BOYS *charge away, they're laughing.* TOM *has turned away, involved, and having lots of fun.*

JOHN. Think it's home time.

MICHAEL. I'm a bit tired.

WENDY *can't stop staring at* TOM.

WENDY (*quietly*). Goodbye, Tom.

She turns and PETER *is in front of her.* PETER *starts being a monkey 'oo-oo'-ing around* WENDY.

Goodbye, Peter.

PETER *stops playing and stands up straight.* WENDY *kisses him on the cheek. There's a squeal, a crow from the* LOST BOYS *and they charge around.* PETER, *for once, doesn't join in – he stares and watches* WENDY *as she joins her brothers, ready to go.*

Ready.

TINK *sprinkles the children with fairy dust and they are up – up and away. Meanwhile, the* LOST BOYS *hoot and play beneath them.* PETER *stands for just one second more.* WENDY *goes to wave to him but he turns, crows and dashes away.*

MICHAEL. Which way, Wendy?

WENDY. Hm?

MICHAEL. Which way do we go?

WENDY. Oh – straight on – no – um – backwards till evening and second on the left.

As the children fly away from Neverland, they hear the wild crowing of PETER PAN *singing through the air.*

Scene Three

In the Darling house – MR DARLING sits alone in the nursery; the house is in a mess. MRS DARLING enters, she is carrying a small holdall and wearing her hat and coat. She turns on a lamp.

MRS DARLING. Boy, why are you crying?

MR DARLING (*with total delight*). Mary?

> MRS DARLING *takes off her hat and puts down her bag.* MR DARLING *starts dashing about, trying to straighten himself out – tidying up and trying to pull some sort of clothing on over his long johns. He ends up with a very floral rug around him, looking quite daft and pacing manically.*
>
> Now – look, Mary – I know you've joined the other side. I know it – so if you've come back here to mock me or kidnap me or throw me out – I – I – I – shall – I shall – I'm not without reason but I shall –

MRS DARLING. George – /

MR DARLING. / I shall be amenable to all your requests – I shall cook more and – and – I shall learn how to do that clothes-flattening thing – even though it seems a very difficult thing to master, I have no idea how you do it /

MRS DARLING. / George.

MR DARLNG. / I shall learn what to order and from where and I would be delighted if you could teach me some recipes, it occurs to me that it is quite ridiculous that I don't know how to make the food that I eat – (*Looks about him, self-consciously.*) which I realise is proven by this disgusting display of cake and crackers /

MRS DARLING. / George!

MR DARLING. Mary – please – please understand – that I do not want you here through duty, it has been my privilege that a woman such as you has chosen to live alongside me and more – chosen to be my wife. Such a privilege, the kind I never dreamed of as a young man – and yet I allowed myself to take that choice for granted and for that I will always be sorry, very sorry indeed. I have only ever wanted you here through love and love alone.

MRS DARLING. Oh, George.

MR DARLING. But I do understand that if you feel you have to go and join those suffragette women and have them come here and tie me up and burn me at the stake or whatever it is that they do – then – then – then I suppose you must and I shall take my punishment like a man.

MRS DARLING. George!

MR DARLING. Yes, Mary?

MRS DARLING. You are crying.

MR DARLING. Yes I am.

MRS DARLING. I don't suppose I've ever seen you cry.

MR DARLING *wipes his tears on the back of his sleeve – he looks like a little boy for a moment.*

MR DARLING. I thought you had gone, I thought I'd lost you.

MRS DARLING. Gone? Never.

MR DARLING. But you took your dresses. You went to join them, to join the march. I thought you might have been arrested or – worse /

MRS DARLING. / What gave you that idea?

MR DARLING *sees the newspaper in* MRS DARLING's *bag and lifts it out – the headline still blazing.*

(*Taking the paper off* MR DARLING *and turning it over to show him an advert circled in red on the back.*) An opening for a seamstress in King's Cross, I took my dresses so I could show them what I was capable of. They kept me several hours for a trial and then afterwards we just talked – talked and talked of fascinating things, George – of the rights for workers and suffragettes and education and /

MR DARLING. / Mary /

MRS DARLING. / Now before you get angry, it is only two days a week and I can still take the children to school and pick them up afterwards /

MR DARLING. / Mary /

MRS DARLING. / And have time to manage the household and the little extra money means you can stop working extra cases /

MR DARLING. / Mary /

MRS DARLING. / It means we'll be spending more time together, not less.

Long silence. MR DARLING *looks at* MRS DARLING.

MR DARLING. I don't care one bit. I am happy – more than happy – look at you – look!

MRS DARLING. What?

MR DARLING. You have your smile back. You have your smile!

MRS DARLING. And you have yours.

MR DARLING. Hello, old friend, I have missed you. I had almost forgotten how – how – (*Thumps his chest.*) how much it makes me want to dance to see you smile!

MR DARLING *sweeps* MRS DARLING *up in his arms and begins to waltz her round the room.*

MRS DARLING. George – you're mad!

MR DARLING. Mad! Mad! Mad!

They whoop and whoosh around the room – laughing. They come to a stop and look at each other softly.

I am so sorry for making you pretend to feel better than you did. To make you go to those infernal parties. I went to see Mrs Bennett when you were gone to check if you might be there.

MRS DARLING. Oh?

MR DARLING. And she spoke about her bonnet for forty-three minutes. I thought about taking her life… with a spatula.

MRS DARLING (*laughing*). And I am sorry for not trying a little harder to be happy. I found it so tricky to keep my upper lip stiff.

MR DARLING. Oh no, it's just perfectly smooshy as it is.

MRS DARLING (*looking at* MR DARLING*'s absurd moustache*). I'm not sure your stiff upper lip suits you all that much?

MR DARLING. I grew it so that people wouldn't see if it began to wobble a bit.

MRS DARLING. Well, perhaps it is time to get rid of it?

MR DARLING. You really don't like it?

MRS DARLING. I think if we wait much longer it might turn into a butterfly.

MR DARLING *kisses* MRS DARLING *strongly*. MR DARLING *picks* MRS DARLING *up and spins her round and round*.

MR DARLING. Let us go out! Let us get the children and go out! We can go skating!

MRS DARLING. I've missed them all day, are they playing in the parlour?

MR DARLING *freezes*.

MR DARLING. No, you took them with you – I presumed they were at your mother's – I –

MRS DARLING. No! I left them sleeping here this morning; I said there was breakfast on the table.

MR DARLING. I thought you meant for me! I checked – I'm sure, I looked in but the nursery was empty – I –

MRS DARLING. George!

MR *and* MRS DARLING *alarmed, start searching the nursery – the bathroom, in cupboards. They both look under the beds for just enough time for the window to fly open and for* WENDY, MICHAEL *and* JOHN *to arrive back, so that they are standing, smiling sweetly, when their parents pop their heads up from under the bed.* MR *and* MRS DARLING *swoop in and scoop them up with hugs and kisses.*

MR DARLING. There you are!

MRS DARLING. Oh my lovely children. Come here!

JOHN. We were fighting pirates!

MICHAEL. And I led a whole army of fireflies!

WENDY. And I organised a whole battle! I flew, Mother, I flew!

JOHN. Were we gone long? Was it years? Did you miss us terribly?

MR DARLING. It was a whole day.

The children laugh.

MRS DARLING. You see – now it is almost dark. I am so glad of you all… and relived that you are safe.

MRS DARLING *shoots a slightly accusatory look at* MR DARLING.

MR DARLING. Come on – we are going to go skating and then we will stop somewhere fancy for cake.

MRS DARLING. And then we shall come home and sit by the fire and tell stories.

WENDY. I am so pleased you and Father are smiling.

MRS DARLING. I am sorry we didn't do it sooner.

MR DARLING. And I am sorry it has been hidden by this silly thing! It shall be gone by morning.

JOHN. I, for one, Father, am very glad – it was getting close to the point where I was going to have to say something.

MR DARLING. Oh God. Yikes.

JOHN. Well, yes, actually.

MICHAEL. Let's go and play!

MR DARLING *takes* JOHN *and* MICHAEL *in a big hug and scoops them up –* JOHN *also puts his arms right around his father with relief.*

MR DARLING. Mary – let's go.

MRS DARLING *wants to follow them but looks anxiously back at the window thinking there might just be one more child to fly through, she can't quite tear herself away.*

MRS DARLING. You go; I'll be down in just a minute.

Beat.

MR DARLING. Last one downstairs is a jibbering jubber dummy!

JOHN. Father? How did you know that you wanted Mother to iron your handkerchiefs?

MR DARLING. Don't wait too long.

MR DARLING *leaves with* MICHAEL *and* JOHN. WENDY *tugs on* MRS DARLING's *dress.*

WENDY. It's all right to come and have some fun.

MRS DARLING. I am, I will – I just –

WENDY. I saw Tom and I – um /

MRS DARLING. / You did?

WENDY. He's having fun. We have to stop waiting.

MRS DARLING. Yes.

WENDY. We must remember to be happy so he can be happy too.

MRS DARLING. Wendy Darling, when did you become so grown up?

WENDY. I'd like to stay little for as long as the boys, if that's all right?

MRS DARLING. Oh – um – well, yes. You should certainly try, but I fear it might… ah – I see.

WENDY. What?

MRS DARLING (*smiles, knowingly*). There – in the corner of your mouth.

WENDY (*blushes and puts her hand over her mouth*). I don't know what you mean.

MRS DARLING *looks down at her daughter with such sympathy – she understands exactly – she gives* WENDY *a big hug*.

MRS DARLING. No more looking after other people, do you hear? You are not to have one more thought about me or your father, or the boys – not one. It is my turn to look after you.

WENDY. All right.

MRS DARLING *spots something in* WENDY's *pocket*.

MRS DARLING. What on earth is that? Look, it is your old thimble but it's glowing, it's covered in some sort of dust?

WENDY. He must have put it in my pocket – I knew he'd kept it! I knew he remembered! I knew it mattered! (*Jigs and does a little dance.*) Oh, boys! They're so silly!

MRS DARLING. That they are.

WENDY *looks at the thimble – a little sad*.

Your heart will mend… I promise… in time.

WENDY. Shall I show you how to fight pirates?

MRS DARLING. Yes!

MRS DARLING *draws one of* JOHN's *swords on* WENDY.

WENDY. Draw your sword, you blundering blubberous buccaneer!

MRS DARLING. You don't stand a chance, you swaggering swine!

Mother and daughter clash, laughing vigorously as they go – leaping up high and rolling around on the ground.

MICHAEL/JOHN/MR DARLING. Come on, you two! Hurry up!

MRS DARLING *races out of the room, pulling on her coat. WENDY looks at the thimble one last time. She goes as if she is going to look out the window, but no – instead she pulls on her coat and runs out after her mother. The nursery is empty – and yet… at the window… if you look hard enough, there's half a shimmer, for just a second, of a flying boy with spiky hair.*

End.

THE HOUND OF THE BASKERVILLES
Steven Canny & John Nicholson
Adapted from Arthur Conan Doyle

THE JUNGLE BOOK
Stuart Paterson
Adapted from Rudyard Kipling

KENSUKE'S KINGDOM
Stuart Paterson
Adapted from Michael Morpurgo

KES
Lawrence Till
Adapted from Barry Hines

NOUGHTS & CROSSES
Dominic Cooke
Adapted from Malorie Blackman

PERSUASION
Mark Healy
Adapted from Jane Austen

THE RAILWAY CHILDREN
Mike Kenny
Adapted from E. Nesbit

SENSE AND SENSIBILITY
Mark Healy
Adapted from Jane Austen

SWALLOWS AND AMAZONS
Helen Edmundson and Neil Hannon
Adapted from Arthur Ransome

TREASURE ISLAND
Stuart Paterson
Adapted from Robert Louis Stevenson

THE WIND IN THE WILLOWS
Mike Kenny
Adapted from Kenneth Grahame

WOLF HALL *and* BRING UP THE BODIES
Mike Poulton
Adapted from Hilary Mantel

A Nick Hern Book

Wendy & Peter Pan first published in Great Britain in 2013 as a paperback original by Nick Hern Books Limited, The Glasshouse, 49a Goldhawk Road, London W12 8QP, in association with the Royal Shakespeare Company

Wendy & Peter Pan copyright © 2013 Ella Hickson

Ella Hickson has asserted her right to be identified as the author of this adaptation

This adaptation of *Peter Pan* by J.M. Barrie published with permission from Great Ormond Street Hospital Children's Charity

Cover image by Rohan Eason with hand-lettering by RSC Visual Communications
Cover design by Ned Hoste, 2H

Typeset by Nick Hern Books, London
Printed and bound in Great Britain by CPI Group (UK) Ltd

A CIP catalogue record for this book is available from the British Library

ISBN 978 1 84842 377 0